creating a
Prodigal-
Friendly
CHURCH

creating a

Prodigal-Friendly CHURCH

JEFF LUCAS

ZONDERVAN.com/
AUTHORTRACKER
follow your favorite authors

Creating a Prodigal-Friendly Church
Copyright © 2008 by Jeff Lucas

Requests for information should be addressed to:
Zondervan, Grand Rapids, Michigan 49530

Library of Congress Cataloging-in-Publication Data

Lucas, Jeff, 1956 –
    Creating a prodigal-friendly church / Jeff Lucas.
        p. cm.
    ISBN-13: 978-0-310-26724-9 (softcover)
    ISBN-10: 0-310-26724-2 (softcover)
    1. Church attendance. 2. Church work with ex-church members. 3. Ex-church members. 4. Church membership. I. Title.
BV652.5.L83 2008
253 – dc22

                                                            2007045561

Interior design by Michelle Espinoza

Printed in the United States of America

08 09 10 11 12 13 • 23 22 21 20 19 18 17 16 15 14 13 12 11 10 9 8 7 6 5 4 3 2 1

*To the Timberline family, who has repeatedly said
one word that changes everything.
Yes.*

CONTENTS

ACKNOWLEDGMENTS

My grateful thanks to Dary and Bonnie Northrop, for friendship, ten thousand conversations, shared laughter, and, at times, shared tears.

Professor Kenneth E. Bailey of Yale Divinity School has spent many years living in the Near East and researching the culture of the New Testament period, especially the background to Luke 15. His work has been invaluable in the writing of this book.

Thanks to my patient and long-suffering editor, John Sloan, and the Zondervan team on both sides of the Atlantic.

Special thanks to the wonderful (but much rained-upon) people at Hillsborough Bible Week, who, through smiles and then emails, prayed and encouraged me through the final ten days of writing ...

And as ever, to my lovely wife, Kay, for her unfailing love and encouragement, especially when it seemed that this book would never be completed.

Chapter 1

OVERTURE: GRACE AND MR. PERLMAN

Overture: Introduction to an opera or other musical work.

*"Grace 'tis a charming sound, harmonious to mine ear,
heaven with the echo shall resound, and all the earth shall hear ..."*
PHILIP DODDRIDGE[1]

You could call it the Miracle on West 65th Street. According to the *Houston Chronicle*, it happened at that address, in New York's Lincoln Center, during a violin concerto.[2]

The concert hall was bustling with warm, preperformance hubbub before the announcer spoke. *Ladies and gentlemen, kindly take your seats now; this evening's performance will begin in two minutes.* People glanced at tickets and hurried to find their rows. They edged their way down the narrow lines of seats to find, at last, their allotted places. *Excuse me. Thank you. You're welcome. Is this my seat?*

Miracles often come without warning or fanfare, and this time was no exception. There was no hint that they were all on the threshold of an experience that they would never forget, a moment to celebrate decades later.

The purposeful din of the orchestra's tuning faded and the lights dimmed, hushing a thousand conversations. The audience was eager for the concert to begin, ready to savor the talents of Itzhak Perlman, arguably the world's greatest violinist.

Perlman is usually the last person to take his place on stage, for though his fingers are staggeringly nimble, his legs don't work nearly as well. He was struck with polio when he was just twelve, and now he struggled across the huge platform to take his seat, his stumbling, ungainly walk aided by crutches and leg braces.

At last, he sat down, removed both braces from his legs, and placed his violin beneath his chin. He was ready—and in more ways than one. Perlman's brilliance is no fluke. He practices for nine hours daily. And for forty-five minutes before every concert, he is alone in his dressing room, with two security guards at the locked door. They have explicit instructions to let no one in under any circumstances. *Mr. Perlman has finished practicing. Now he is praying. Do not disturb.*

And pray he must. The concerto is considered one of the most important and difficult works in the violin repertoire. Its technical demands on the soloist are huge. Brahms' *Violin Concerto in D Major* is simply "unplayable" according to one virtuoso. That miracle night, Perlman was set to perform this extraordinarily challenging piece that would last over six minutes.

A few seconds into the solo, the sound of a string breaking on Perlman's violin ricocheted around the hall. The unwelcome *twang* was an uncouth intruder among a myriad of perfect notes. The orchestra immediately stopped playing, their music tapering off chaotically. The crowd gasped. Protocol permits a musician to call for a pause, allowing time for them to hurry off stage to replace the string. It's quite impossible to play a complicated violin concerto a string short.

Impossible, that is, unless your name is Perlman. With a wave he signaled the orchestra to continue. And then the unthinkable happened.

Instantaneously transposing the music for three strings instead of four, Perlman delivered the piece flawlessly, his dancing fingers producing sounds of unprecedented purity and passion. Six minutes later, spent and soaked in sweat, he lowered his violin. The crowd sat in stunned silence for eight seconds. And then they rose as one to their feet, a wall of wild cheering and thunderous applause. The orchestra joined in, banging their instruments in homage and shouting themselves hoarse. Perlman called for a microphone, motioned for silence, and then the man with two busted legs and one busted string spoke:

"All my life, it has been my mission to make music from that which remains."

His brilliance was expressed through something broken. The shattered string, which could have stopped the music, only served to accentuate Perlman's staggering talent. Greater glory came because the melody-maker used a temporarily useless instrument.

GOD'S GRACE: MUSIC TO OUR EARS

And that is precisely what God has always done with us, creating beautiful music through broken people. How desperately the world needs to hear the charming sound that is grace. There's no shortage of harsh noise on this planet, but rather a famine of real music. Daily our ears and hearts are bombarded with the ominous, deep bass sounds of terrorism and war; we are both tormented and tempted by the shrill ditties of commercialism and perplexed by the monotone, haunting chants of fundamentalism. But there is yet beautiful music to be heard in the universe. God longs for the lilting melody of his love to be heard, true music to the ear for those who have ears to hear it.

Though all of us need to hear this song, prodigals desperately need to hear it. A prodigal is someone who has walked or drifted away from God, sometimes because they've been seduced by another sound. They've heard the Father's love song, but they felt like they were always "facing the music" rather than being wooed by it. Some got bored with the sound; the gospel became repetitive and predictable, like an endless sound loop played while you're on hold, a nagging ditty. Still others heard the song, but pushed it to the background—elevator music.

Others heard it loud and clear, but it didn't seem quite real, like a wedding singer belting out Beatles numbers. Some of them may have been briefly inoculated with a mild dose of vacuous religion, but the vaccination turned bad and they showed God their backs. Marching off to the so-called far country, that place where the thrill rules, where eternity is ignored and the next second is everything, they have lived unconcerned about God's ways and unmoved by his love. Perhaps there have been occasional chats with him over the years, but the call has always been long distance, and usually of the 911 type. Now they want to make the relationship local, not just for emergencies.

And there are other prodigals who have never given God a second thought, but now they can't get him out of their minds, and they're showing up at churches hoping to hear the sound of a welcome-home party. Strictly speaking, perhaps they're not prodigals, but their desire to come in from the cold into the warmth of the kingdom party is wonderful—and deeply challenging, especially for some of us guests who have already been seated around the banqueting table for a while. The prodigals' arrival home creates a reaction. Some of us join in with the welcome party, and some are less happy. There are those who celebrate, and some who rage at their homecoming. Still others are coldly indifferent. *A prodigal is home? Alright, but he'd better fit in, toe the line, and clean up quick.*

When a prodigal comes home, it's an answer to prayer—and the beginning of a potential crisis. The presence of "sinners" made "holy" people feel uncomfortable in Jesus's day. Two thousand years later, the tension continues.

WHY THIS BOOK?

In my first book on this subject, *Will Your Prodigal Come Home?*, I sought to bring words of honesty and hope to those who love prodigals, those who worry and hurt as they wait for a homecoming. I tried to show that we can carry guilt about our prodigals that is not really ours to own. Adam and Eve had the perfect parenting of God—and yet they still walked away. God has always had trouble with his kids. I called us to release our prodigals to come back home to *God*—not to our church, our ways, or our opinions. I celebrated the truth that God truly is the persistent "hound of heaven" out there in the far country, searching out the prodigals: the stories of the lost sheep, the lost coin, and the lost son are all part of but *one* parable. The father who anxiously scans the horizon and then sprints to welcome his son is also the diligent shepherd wandering the bleak hills, looking for those who have told him to get lost and who have gotten lost themselves. His character is explored in yet another story of the woman who turns her house upside down as she searches high and low for a coin and then throws an impromptu party when it's found. I encouraged faith-filled prayer for the return of our prodigals and offered some words that can be used as prayers to those whose pain has rendered them speechless.

But all our hoping and praying will be to no avail if prodigals return to churches that are efficient, "prodigal-making" machines. Speaking recently at a conference about reaching prodigals, Rob Parsons put it memorably: "We need to pray that the returning prodigals will meet the Father before they bump into the elder brother."[3] We urgently need prodigal-friendly churches for but one reason: prodigals matter.

Right now, as your eyes pass over this print, tens of thousands of so-called prodigals are thinking about taking a hike home to God. Their fun ran out with their money—or maybe money couldn't buy enough fun—and now they're bored, scared, lonely, and empty. They deserve a boisterous welcome party that they could never earn. Will we surprise them with love?

And at this very moment, there are people who love prodigals, who are aching terribly, haunted by worry, some of them jumpy and fearful every time the phone rings. Perhaps you are one of them. There are parents, siblings, aunts, uncles, grandparents, and friends who are weeping for prodigals, desperately praying that they will come safely home. It hurts like hell (I use the phrase thoughtfully) to love a prodigal. God forbid that the prayers of those so broken and bruised would be sabotaged by someone like the loud, aggressive big brother in the story, a pious party pooper who wants to pull the plug on the band and save the fatted calf for a "nicer" occasion. Those who cry for prodigals matter.

But there's another very good reason for us to consider what it means to be prodigal-friendly: The prodigals utterly matter to *God*. He skips for joy when they come home to him and he sobs with anguished rage when they don't find a welcome at the kingdom table. He is passionate. It's cold out there, and God cries for those lost in the chilly wastelands. This is the God who agonized over Israel and suffered with her suffering. Hosea prophesied about the God who said, "My heart is changed within me"[4] because his people provoked and grieved him.[5] Becoming prodigal-friendly is not a heartless mechanism to accelerate our church growth potential, to ensure that our numerical expansion is in line with our projections. Away with that kind of language, for this is enough: *prodigals matter.*

Being prodigal-friendly is about developing a heart for prodigals and looking to create a culture that is friendly to them, one that might have prevented them from walking away in the first place. That's no mean feat, especially as the church — the churches that you and I are part of — change and shift every second of the day. As words are spoken, attitudes develop, relationships ebb and flow, new people come and others leave, sermons are preached and prayers are prayed, so every church changes. Being prodigal-friendly is not about getting a logo of approval that states you are hereby "officially" pronounced as church friendly to prodigals. Rather, we must pray that God will allow us to catch glimpses and hints of what it means to have his heart for those who've decided to walk away.

And so through this book, let's consider the feel, the texture, if you will, of a prodigal-friendly church. To do that, we'll be using Jesus's beautiful story of the lost son (or perhaps, more accurately, the parable of the good father and his two lost sons) as a "house" to live in for a while.

THE POWER OF PARABLE

Permit me a word about our use of parable. We all know that Jesus loved to tell stories — it was his preferred method of teaching.

These wonderful stories were not designed to dumb down truth, but rather to provoke thought, discussion, and heart searching.

A parable is not a vehicle to convey one single truth, for a number of ideas can be expressed beautifully through story. But we tread into dangerous territory here. Preachers through the years have subjected the parables to endless allegorizing, which is unfortunate, and has prompted some theologians to insist that a parable has only one core idea at its heart. But surely, Jesus, metaphorical theologian that he was, invites us to live in the story. It's been said that to rightly understand a parable, we must treat it like a house with many rooms.

The story of the lost son is packed full with vital truth; no wonder Latin tradition called it "the gospel within the gospel." Here we see who we are, when we are at our best, and when we are at our worst. What we see isn't encouraging. Humans don't do well either as sinners or would-be saints. How easily we are attracted by the slightest scent of sin; how frequently we tumble headlong into the pit of dead, heartless religion.

And then, in just a few words, we see what God is like and we sigh with relief. He is like the smitten father who anxiously scans the horizon, looking for the crazy, mixed-up kid that is me and you both. I pray that by the end of our journey, we will not only have been moved by this lovely story, but by much more.

For this tale is no fiction. We won't taste the flat disappointment when the theater lights come up as the play or movie ends and we realize we have been captivated by a fabricated myth. How often have we had to face the truth that a story's hero is simply an actor, one who in real life has a drug problem and has been less than heroic in his relationships. As we look at the father in the story of the prodigal son, however, we know that there truly *is* a love like his in the universe, for there is a God and he is for real.

One more word is needed, because *how* we travel is as important as *where* we will go. I write this book as a learner and fellow traveler. I may become excessively passionate, even angry at times at what I see us as a church doing—and not doing. Ironically, I can become like the prodigal's big brother—angry at my fellow brothers and sisters. I love the church and respect her deeply. I write as one who wants to build up, not destroy. There is no shortage of voices that endlessly bray on about the shortcomings of the church, but who don't offer many answers. God forbid that you or I should become like Lucy in the Charlie Brown cartoon, who states, "The whole trouble with you, Charlie Brown, is that you're you!" Understandably, Charlie responds, "Well, what in the world can I do about it?" Lucy's reply chills and challenges me: "I don't pretend to be able to give advice; I merely point out the trouble."

We must face some hard questions together. In my home country of England, for every adult in church, four other adults used to attend regularly but have now given up. That adds up to a lot of pain. *Well,* some say, *that's what happens when people make poor choices.* When a person leaves the church and becomes a prodigal, we can be quick to conclude that *they* need to change and return to where *we* are. But we must face the challenge to change and be intentionally prodigal-friendly if we are to prevent people from leaving or help them return. For that to happen, we will need to be humble, generous people who refuse to be defensive about the weaknesses of our churches.

BEAUTIFUL MUSIC FROM AN IMPERFECT ORCHESTRA

As I write, I plan to pause, to repent, to dream, to be grateful, and to pray. Please join me along the way in these activities as we listen once more to that familiar story told about one man who came home and another who remained defiantly outside. Will he stay there?

Our story, that of you and me, is still being written. Will we allow God to shape us into his likeness? Will we bring our gifts to help make the party swing, or will we stay out in the cold night air? Perhaps our first prayer should be to ask God to change our hearts as well as our minds, because the prodigal-friendly church will not be a church with a shiny new strategy, a fail-safe program, or a revival-launching outreach technique. Instead, it will be a church with a compassionate heart that weeps for the prodigals. It will be a brave people willing to be instruments for music that is "unplayable"—unless the Lord plays it through them.

But most of all it will be a church filled with ordinary, "three-stringed" people. Not a Stradivarius in sight, for God only uses the ordinary; nothing else is available. Tarnished trumpets. Big, fat double basses, varnish scratched, a tuning peg or two out of line. Strings encased in rust, brittle to the touch. A dented timpani that *boings* when a *bong* is expected. A flute that squeaks and drips spit. Cymbals that sometimes *zing* rather than *clang*. He uses what he has, what remains. That would be us. Through this motley assortment of dusty, junk shop castoffs, our God, the ultimate composer and musician, can transpose the music once more.

If you are a follower of Jesus, your place is not in the audience, waiting for someone else to play: the prodigal-friendly church will not come about just because some leaders and pastors decide that it should be so. Rather, as each of us offer ourselves afresh as part of the orchestra, the dream of harmonious music making becomes a reality.

What's that I hear? Excuse me, the announcer is calling. Today's performance continues. Places, please, everyone.

Chapter 2

DISSONANCE: THE MUTTERERS

Dissonance: Harsh, discordant, and lacking harmony. Also a chord that sounds incomplete until it resolves itself on a harmonious chord.

Now the tax collectors and "sinners" were all gathering around to hear him. But the Pharisees and the teachers of the law muttered, "This man welcomes sinners and eats with them." Then Jesus told them this parable...
LUKE 15:1–3

"He touched untouchables with love and washed the guilty clean..."
COMMUNION SERVICE, COMMON WORSHIP[1]

Perhaps they had lingered in the lengthening shadows to catch him leaving the house at the end of a meal. Surely they wanted to witness his scandalous behavior firsthand.

The men waiting outside had carefully tracked his movements for some days now, an easy task in such a small community, where news, especially bad news, travels fast. They'd analyzed the plentiful intelligence chatter, for their target was making a huge impact everywhere and there was no shortage of eyewitnesses. His public statements, outrageous and provocative, were well documented. And though his speeches were shocking—one never knew what turn he would take when he opened his mouth in public—their suspect was fairly predictable in his movements. He'd developed quite the reputation as a socialite and was fast becoming an A-list celebrity, a guest in demand. And he could usually be found hanging out in the wrong part of town.

That night, he'd been at yet another dinner party, but, as far as the whispering huddle of men outside were concerned, it was no glittering affair. Perhaps they'd scanned the guest list and scowled. A rancid collection of lowlifes and losers had dined with him, but this was hardly a beggar's banquet. Granted, there were a few small-time crooks who barely scratched a living from their scavenging, and a handful of nobodies who were usually short on invites and grabbed any opportunity for a free meal. But a couple of big-time operators tucked into the hearty meal too. Well-fed and well-heeled, they were accomplished extortionists, experts at pilfering other people's wallets. The men who waited outside were stunned that he dignified this uncouth gaggle with his company. Frankly, his actions were treacherous. Nothing less than national security was at stake. Something had to be done.

Outside, the men had waited patiently for him to show his face, enduring the numbing boredom of the stakeout, but eager to gather more evidence and personally confirm the rumor mill. Perhaps they stomped their feet against the evening chill. They would have been increasingly angered by the peals of laughter that drifted out from within. Did they step back into the blackness of an alley to avoid being spotted as some guests hurried away early? Did they encourage each other in their patient contempt, muttering behind cupped hands?

Suddenly, without warning, he appeared in the doorway, a couple of his closest friends at his side. The ambushers stopped their mumbling and just stared, accusing eyes narrowed. So the rumors were true. It *was* him. Within seconds, he disappeared into the night.

THE PRODIGAL PRESS RELEASE

"He," of course, is Jesus, and those pursuing him were Pharisees and other critics, eager to stop his outrageous behavior. The next day, Jesus was at the center of yet another commotion, the crowds hanging onto his every word. Crying children were hushed, chatterers frowned at. He was the darling of these common people, or so it seemed. But not everyone was a fan. On the edge of the group, at a distance calculated to say, *We're spectating, not joining in*, stood a quietly enraged cluster. It was the same men who had watched and waited outside last night. They scanned his adoring audience, their eyes a mixture of mockery and disgust. What a pathetic herd of no-hopers he'd gathered. Jesus's poker-faced critics were appalled to spot a couple of treacherous collaborators listening in; they also sat a little apart from the rest of the crowd, but for very different reasons. They knew they were despised by all, tagged as quislings.

Not only did he teach these people, "the scum of the earth," but now they knew from their investigation the previous evening that he ate with them too. As far as the little group of angry men were concerned, that made him just as bad as his roughneck dining companions. He was guilty by association.

Did he hear their muttering? Or did he instinctively know exactly what was on their minds?

Without warning, Jesus issued a statement. Or, to be more accurate, he told them a story. It didn't help assuage their anger; on the contrary, it fueled their fire. As the simple but shocking plotline unfolded, they exchanged dark glances, as if to say, *Can you believe this stuff?* His story got two thumbs down.

The marvelous little tale that Jesus told is more like a press release issued during a crisis than a familiar homily. It's packed with suspense and sudden hairpin turns. As we'll see later, the tale of two sons and their father would have been utterly shocking to Near Eastern ears, so unexpected was the behavior of all three characters.

One, the younger and infamous prodigal son, embodies the utter madness, the blinding insanity that seeps into our souls and shrouds our minds when greed becomes our god, when we decide that there's only one line worth embracing as a life mantra: *Give me*. Everything goes south for that young kid hell-bent on a good time. Steely-eyed, he demands his family inheritance. This was more than bad manners—his request meant that he was effectively wishing his father dead. With his newly acquired assets hurriedly turned into cash, the lad heads for the beckoning bright lights. After some breakneck high-roller living, he blows the lot, and ends up out of money, friends, and luck. Once well fed, once a son and heir, now he is reduced to being a gaunt hobo, desperate and scrabbling to survive. He tumbles to shocking depths. Finally, with nowhere else to go, he heads wearily for home, but not for any noble reasons. He craves a square meal and hopes for a job. Even his dad's employees have a life far better than his. Homeward bound, he's not a pretty sight.

Look at the state of him. Has he been living in a dumpster? His eyes are sunken, black holes gouged deep by too many backbreaking days and sleepless nights. His skin is pallid and pockmarked, encrusted with grime. His teeth are filthy, his breath fetid from making garbage his diet.

His shoes are rotting off his feet, splattered with the mustard yellow of aged manure, held together by a thread of leather here and there. His fingernails are caked black with dirt, his hair tangled and spotted with lice, and there's no family signet ring on his bony fingers—it's long gone, pawned for food years back. A sweat-stained, threadbare robe hangs lank upon his bowed shoulders. The air is filled with the stale odor of a long-unwashed body. He stinks to high heaven.

But what a surprise awaits him.

As the returning prodigal becomes a growing dot on the horizon, Dad appears, kindness and grace on legs. His unrequited love has longed and watched for him for years, and when at last he catches sight of his exhausted son, love picks up its skirts and goes running. The lad's father is utterly thrilled that his nighttime fears of his boy lying dead in some far-off alley are all wrong. The red carpet is rolled out. Friends and neighbors are hastily summoned for a spontaneous, epic bash. Top sirloin hits the grill, there's a prodigal gift shower, the band strikes up a merry tune, and the dancing begins. If this were a movie, the orchestra would be soaring into happy overdrive; we'd dab our eyes and feel all warm within.

It's so wonderful to see you, lad. Raise your glasses, friends: another toast, the long-lost boy is found, home now at last. The place is hopping, a heaving morass of happiness, and everybody, with the notable exception of the fattened calf, is thrilled.

Strike that. Not everybody. Just as we thought the words *The End* were to appear on the screen, the happy reunion is cut short by a knife-edge twist in the plot.

There's a commotion outside the house, the sound of angry yelling. A servant rushes in, urgently calling his master's name. *It's an emergency. Come quickly. Is someone hurt? Has one of the guests overindulged with the wine and wound up at the center of a drunken spat?* Father rushes outside, perhaps flanked by a throng of eager spectators who sense trouble and don't want to miss a potentially delicious spectacle.

A family fight at a party is excruciatingly embarrassing. Too many beautiful occasions have been wrecked by raised voices and flying fists, the soft magic of the occasion shattered in seconds by a flurry of rough words quickly spoken—and regretted for years. To everyone's amazement, it's the older son, renowned for his faithfulness and solid character, now yelling at his father, an appalling crime in the culture of the day. Like his kid brother, his clothes are filthy too, but they are soiled with the honest sweat of supervising a long day's work on the farm. His arms are folded, locked solid in defiance; his eyes are razor-narrow slits of blazing rage. He plants his feet, arrogant, unmovable, absolutely in the right—or so he thinks. He is furious. A nervous informant has told him the reason for the unscheduled party, and now he trembles with rage and bunches his fists, his whitened knuckles ready to pummel someone. Anyone will do as a punching bag. His face contorts, an ugly mask, and his words come out staccato, spat rather than spoken; verbal venom.

His father is anxious. He approaches his son with a nervous, hopeful smile and outstretched arms, so desperate is he to broker peace. An arm now around his son's shoulder, he pleads with words and eyes. *Please come inside, my dear, dear boy. The lad is* here—*your brother. The dead live. We all thought he was long gone, but wonder of wonders, he's safe and sound, home at last. Come in, cherished son of mine. Eat, drink, and be merry. It's party time.*

No. The answer is *no.*

Not on your life, old man. This is an outrage, an obscene charade. That useless scumbag, so-called son of yours has royally ripped off the whole family. His boozy binges and whore-mongering have cost everyone dearly. He's hocked our heirlooms, smeared our good name, and now—unbelievably—he's feasting on the best beef. He's no brother of mine. Count me out, and stand accused of a couple of crimes yourself, Father: you're a mean, ungrateful slave driver, and you're naïve, stupid, and reckless too. Hasn't Junior in there squandered enough of the family fortune? Now you're throwing more of our hard-earned cash down the drain. He's a waster, and so, Father, are you.

Freeze the frame and look again. Inside the house, the band, suddenly silenced by the fracas, stands poised to strike up another merry tune so that the joyous stomping can continue. But outside, a father pleads with his oldest son, perhaps tearfully. *Please. We had to celebrate. It was the right thing—the only thing—to do.*

Here is a party, and here is a fight. The bout is between the grace of God and the big-brother attitude. Some things never change.

JOY AND ANGER IN THE "HAPPY FAMILY" CHURCH

Timberline Church (known then as First Assembly of God, Fort Collins) was propelled, overnight, into a similar crisis about fifteen years ago. Described by senior pastor Dary Northrop as a "happy family" church, Timberline was steadily growing, with over five hundred people attending. It was Dary and Bonnie Northrop's first appointment as senior leaders. They had previously served successfully as youth pastors, but now they were in uncharted territory. Did they have what it took to take the reins of a church and steer it forward? Their fledgling leadership skills were about to be stretched to the limit. Then, one fine day, Nicky showed up.

Nicky was an extremely bright and beautiful law student, and she had developed a novel plan to pay her way through college. Nicky was a stripper. She'd decided that if men were stupid enough to part with cash—lots of it—to encourage her to take her clothes off, then so be it; she'd take their money willingly and part with her clothes "artistically." She was a high earner.

Nicky had her hair and nails done by Larry, a beautician who attended First Assembly. After a while, she noticed that there was something quite different about Larry because, unlike most other men she'd ever met, he never tried to hit on her. Intrigued, she asked him why he'd shown no interest. He had a different value system, he said, and he wouldn't treat her like that. Nicky was fascinated by this man who saw her as more than skin or an object of conquest. He talked gently and movingly about his faith in Jesus Christ, but without the pushy arrogance that smites some people who've got religion and want to force-feed it to everyone else. Nicky wanted to go to church with Larry, but at first he refused, telling her that she wasn't ready, a novel evangelistic approach—and one that worked. She insisted, and so the following Sunday morning they sat in balcony seats at First Assembly—for all of about two minutes. Restless, Nicky wanted to sit in the front row downstairs, right in the middle of the action. And so Larry and Nicky moved pews and drew a few stares as they walked down the center aisle. Though not dressed inappropriately, Nicky wasn't wearing anything that would pass for church-lady attire. She sat wide-eyed as Dary preached. He was talking directly to her, or so it seemed. She kept nudging Larry and whispering too loudly. "Why did you tell him I was coming today?" she hissed. "He knows all about me. How come? What did you tell him?" Behind a cupped hand, red-faced Larry tried to hiss assurances to Nicky that Dary had not been tipped off. Why, he had no idea that she was going to be there that day. Obviously God had set Nicky up with an appointment with destiny and, more importantly, with himself. At the end of the sermon, Dary invited people who didn't know Christ to make a public commitment to him. Nicky's was the first hand raised in response.

What happened next was really rather wonderful—and traumatic. A few days into the following week, Nicky called Dary at home. Dary was a little taken aback, as he wasn't used to receiving phone calls from strippers. Nicky asked Dary if he read the Bible much. He said he did. She'd read the entire New Testament through in just a few days. Nicky asked Dary if he had read that part in the Bible about the human body being the temple of the Holy Spirit, which of course he had. "Jesus doesn't want me to use my body like this, to be a stripper, does he?" Nicky asked nervously. Dary agreed, answering her questions rather than pushing her to conclusions. Then Nicky asked if Dary was familiar with those verses in the Bible where God promises to take care of us, as he does the birds of the air and the lilies of the field. Nicky, burdened with a large college loan and living costs and with no other visible means of support, asked if Jesus would take care of her if she gave up stripping. With a gulp, Dary said yes, he was convinced that God would honor that decision.

It was enough. Nicky went back to the strip joint and, without being preachy or condemnatory, told her employers and friends of her decision. She wept as she talked about Jesus and invited them all to come to her baptism. They agreed, closing the club for the evening. I'm sure that disappointed customers did not see a sign on the club door that read, "Strip show cancelled due to baptism," but it's a delicious thought.

Nicky and thirteen of her friends strode down the aisle that Sunday night. The sight of them caused quite the stir in that "happy family" church. Some of the women with Nicky obviously—very obviously—believed that bras were optional. Ladies in halter tops and skirts split up to the thigh are fairly scarce in churches. On display were chains, leather, a few dozen metal piercings, and a variety of colorful tattoos. Some of the "happy family" church wives covered their husbands' eyes as the gang of fourteen took their seats.

Around eight from that group became Christians that night, surely a reason to rejoice. Turn up that party music and pass those poppers around, because lost people have been found. Fire up the barbecue. This was what that church had been praying for, and this was the reason they'd sacrificed heavily to build their church building into a facility to help them to reach their community. Didn't they all believe in a Bible that talks about the sheer exhilaration in the presence of the angels when one sinner comes home to God? And indeed there was a real sense of excitement that swept through the church. Late night Bible studies began, scheduled at midnight to nurture the people from the club scene. The unique joy that can only be experienced by a church with baby Christians around was in the air.

But babies, to put it bluntly, also make very bad smells. Not everybody in that "happy family" church was happy now.

YOU'VE RUINED THIS CHURCH

Walking down the corridor to his office one day, Dary was accosted by one of the ladies of the church who'd been around for years. She was committed to God, faithful to First Assembly—and extremely angry. She jabbed an accusatory finger at Dary. "You've ruined this church," she snarled. She wasn't at all pleased about the newcomers—on the contrary. She was wrestling with some real issues coupled, undeniably, with some bad attitudes. One of the "happy family" church children had been scratched on the face by one of the children of the newcomers—and that's a genuine problem. And then the complaining lady was genuinely worried about the good name, the "testimony," of First Assembly. Would outsiders think that, because people of very public loose morals were showing up, the church had lost its firm grip on biblical values? She was genuinely concerned about guilt by association. Then there was the issue of the youth group. With an influx of kids fresh from the soft and hard drug scene, who would be influencing whom? There were other, smaller difficulties. The cigarette butts that littered the parking lot. The rumor that one of the "happy church" kids had acquired a tattoo, without his parents' approval. After all, there were quite a few other tattooed folks in the church now.

For her, First Assembly was no longer a safe place: it was filled with people that she didn't know—and didn't want to know. They'd never learned how to behave "in church." It was becoming more difficult to park the car and sit in one's beloved pew. There was a period when all the newcomers sat separately from the happy family folks, obviously distinctive by their fashion choices.

Nervousness continued. Dary recalls the day when one of the established members gave him some cash, pointed across the church building to someone who was clearly in need, and asked him to pass the gift on. "I'm happy to do that," smiled Dary, "but why don't you give him the money yourself?" "No," stammered the agitated but generous giver, "I want to help him, but I don't want to *know* him." The "happy family" had been invaded. Trespassers were not just around, they seemed to be the focus of attention. The more people came, the harder it got to get an appointment with the pastor; the on-call shepherd now had a larger flock to tend. No longer was the church full of people who had invested in relationships over the years, who understood the vision and had invested their time, money, and energy into it. And then some of these new people inevitably drifted away and walked back into their old lifestyles, surely proving that this was not really a "genuine" work of God.

And why were some of these so-called new converts still in the club scene? Shouldn't they be rebuked and told bluntly that if they weren't willing to get their lives sorted out, then they weren't welcome in the church? After all, God wants a holy, pure people for his own.

There was a crisis, and not just because some people struggled with their attitudes. Some were wrestling theologically. The big-brother attitude was growing fast, and some of those who exhibited it the most were the most passionate and radically committed people in the church. Some were fearful, nervous about traveling through this uncharted territory, anxious about taking what seemed like precarious steps. But grace always goes looking for notorious sinners. And when those sinners show up around Jesus — and then, perhaps, around *our* church — it invariably creates a crisis.

Chapter 3

INTERMEZZO: DINING WITH THE PRODIGAL ZACCHAEUS

Intermezzo: A short movement or interlude connecting the main parts of the composition.

"The spirit of Jesus penetrates social boxes. Barricades of suspicion, mistrust, stigma and hate crumble in his presence. He calls us to see the human being behind the stigmatized social labels. His kingdom transcends all boundaries. He welcomes people from all boxes. His love overpowers the social customs which divide, separate and isolate ... The agape of Jesus reaches out to boxed-up people, telling them God's love washes away their stigma and welcomes them into a new community."

DONALD KRAYBILL[1]

He was hated.

Familiar to Sunday school children everywhere as that vertically-challenged chap who scampered up a tree to catch a better view of Jesus, Zacchaeus was not just mildly unpopular because he was a taxman. Preachers sometimes paint verbal portraits of Zacchaeus that make him out to be like a mild-mannered but somewhat intimidating-looking guy from the IRS who lives down the street. People give him a wide berth, more because of fear than reason.

For Zacchaeus, it was worse than that. Much worse.

He was a social pariah, someone to shun. *Quick, cross the street, here he comes.* With the exception of his slimy cohorts in the tax trade, most people loathed him. Every day he would have seen the silent, seething hatred in their eyes as they handed over their hard-earned cash without a word. There was no hiding the contempt they felt, and theirs was not just a rage against the oppressive Roman machine. It was personal. They hated *him*.

All tax gatherers were viewed as collaborators with the occupying forces, "lackeys of Rome."[2] Zacchaeus had sold his soul for a buck. He'd tossed his Jewish identity aside so he could fleece his own people and line his own pockets. He had kicked them all while they were down. For the common people, life was already an uphill grind, a never-ending fight to survive. Zacchaeus made their plight much worse, bleeding them dry like a leech. As they reluctantly pressed their coins into his clammy, ever-open hand, they knew he was taking them for far more than they owed. And so they wrote him off, the worst of a bad bunch.

The so-called "sinners," the untouchables of Jesus's day, were those who practiced one of the seven despised trades, which included barbers, tanners, and (interesting in the light of the nativity) shepherds. There were others, those considered guilty of flagrant immorality—the prostitutes, adulterers, gamblers, and murderers. They made the list, as did those who refused to observe the Law according to the Pharisees' understanding of it. All Gentiles were written off en masse too.

But at the very top of the list of shame were the tax collectors, which is why the Bible gives them special mention when it singles them out by saying that Jesus was a friend of *tax collectors* and sinners.[3] When a story was needed to contrast a seeming saint with a hopeless sinner, Jesus chose the characters of a Pharisee and a tax collector as two extreme opposites.[4]

Tradition taught that if a tax collector entered any house, the food and the premises were rendered unclean by their presence,[5] a kind of human virus. You can't redeem a germ, or so it was thought. Tax gatherers were viewed as utterly beyond redemption. It was taught that repentance was impossible for them,[6] which made Jesus's repeated statements about one of the tax gatherers being a "son of Abraham" and another "justified before God" especially shocking.[7] Ironically, Zacchaeus's name meant "clean and innocent," a fact that must have sparked many cruel jokes.

Just to make matters worse, Zacchaeus was a *chief* tax collector. The Romans had turned taxation into a franchise business, allowing seedy entrepreneurs to bid for the opportunity to control a territory. The *chiefs* ran a number of agents, paying them on a commission basis. The more they collected, the more they made. And the chief was the fat cat who took plenty of cream for himself. He was a hated head honcho.

So this was the little man perched up in the branches, small in stature, big in power, and tiny in terms of social worth: a wretched, rotten nobody. And one who, for some reason, wanted to catch a glimpse of Jesus. And here comes Jesus now.

Look at the crowd. They're a jostling, shoving, dangerous morass, each of them eager for the best view of Jesus, this strange, wonderful man. There's no way Zacchaeus is going to try his luck — or tempt his fate — in the middle of that lot. An attempt to find a space in the throng could leave him vulnerable to a solid punch to his kidneys, or worse. And his height — or lack of it — meant that he'd miss everything if he just stood quietly at the back of the crowd, hence the hasty tree climbing. He had a marvelous view from his spot high in the branches, and he savored the moment until things went terribly wrong ... or right.

Jesus slowed as he approached the sycamore tree, looked up, and stared. At him.

Did a second or two seem like an hour as, terrified, the taxman waited for Jesus to speak? Would Jesus wither Zacchaeus with a razor-sharp sentence that would topple him from the branches and bring him down to earth, literally, with a sickening bump? It's agonizing to be picked out of a crowd, especially when you're the one they love to hate. A public tongue-lashing for the despised chief would have delighted the people.

Jesus spoke Zacchaeus's name. Some say that he knew the little man's name by heavenly revelation. Or perhaps Zacchaeus was simply so infamous that Jesus recognized him perched up there in the tree. However he knew it, the fact that Jesus used Zacchaeus's name matters. Humans are not just objects of discussion to be filed under a category: put him under *S* for sinner. They have names, and hopes, and histories. Zacchaeus was a person. The sound of it on Jesus's lips was surely music to his ears.

But what happened next was like a stun grenade to everyone, not least Zacchaeus.

Jesus invited himself for lunch. Zacchaeus was ecstatic, and practically fell out of the tree with delight. Perhaps we too would love to rush over to the taxman's place, park ourselves in that dining room, and wonder about the warm chatter, the broad smiles, the laughter. We want to zoom in on the marvelous sight of the lifelong extortionist doing a U-turn and becoming a philanthropist. But let's resist the temptation to hurry to that beautiful episode and ponder a more sobering sight instead.

CALLED TO RISKY LOVE

Look at that crowd. Moments earlier they were waiting with cheers of praise for Jesus. Now their faces are rigid with anger, smiles replaced by sneers.

They're muttering and complaining. He's taking tea with a traitor—and not even a repentant one at that. When Jesus gave himself an invitation, there was not a hint of remorse from Zacchaeus; all of that would come much later. So this was risky, even scandalous behavior on Jesus's part. According to Near Eastern culture, sitting at a table with another was an act of intimacy and fellowship—to offer hospitality was to give honor[8] and trusting acceptance. Refusal to share a meal conversely signaled rejection and disapproval. And there were political implications to table fellowship: the meal was a "survival symbol"[9] to a people occupied by a hated force—and now Jesus was apparently diluting that by dining with a traitorous tax chief. Was the Messiah snacking on food that had been put on the taxman's table as a result of his greed and extortion? That would have been a very risky act indeed, almost sharing in his ill-gotten gains, becoming a partner in his crime. The crowd would have expected Jesus to treat "sinners" as everyone else did, socially ostracizing them to deter others from following in their footsteps.

But Jesus practiced a far more creative alternative. Grace, kindness, and the use of a man's name were the prompts to the revolution that overwhelmed Zacchaeus's life. He would never be the same again.

Likewise, we are called to be a people known more for risky love than pious murmuring. When a church decides to be prodigal-friendly, there will always be those—especially other Christians—who will misunderstand and accuse us of becoming liberals, of diluting or ignoring biblical standards of behavior. Grace always offends. A prodigal-friendly church may well create quite a stir, refusing to bow to the social expectations that churches be stacked with apparently nice people. But we must do more than marvel at Jesus's spectacular risk-taking: we are called to emulate him.

In one sense this is no great sacrifice for us, for surely we are only sinners insisting on taking risks with others who are just like us. Jesus was spotless, but hung out with the spotted. We're people still in process, sinners all of us, recovering, being changed, yet journeying still. But we are called to truly follow and imitate him. Being criticized by others who insist that they are not only fellow followers of Christ but more faithful than us "compromisers" will be part of the price of true discipleship.

Catherine Mowry LaCugna describes the costly call:

> Living the Trinitarian faith means living as Jesus Christ lived; preaching the gospel; relying totally upon God; offering healing and reconciliation; rejecting laws, customs and conventions that place people beneath rules; resisting temptation; praying constantly; eating with modern day lepers and other outcasts; embracing the enemy and the sinner; dying for the sake of the gospel if it is God's will.[10]

If we refuse to take that calculated risk, then we risk something far worse—becoming part of a murmuring crowd that prevents people from seeing the real Jesus. And that's not a risk we should be willing to take.

Chapter 4

MANCANDO: ARE WE PREVENTING A PARTING?

Mancando: Fading away.

Jesus continued: "There was a man who had two sons. The younger one said to his father, 'Father, give me my share of the estate.' So he divided his property between them.

Not long after that, the younger son got together all he had, set off for a distant country ..."

A recent survey uncovered a scandal. Nine out of ten people who have walked away from churches were never asked why they left. It's an indictment that so many leavers said that no one seemed to notice they'd gone. That's careless.
LESLIE FRANCIS

So far, so bad.

The younger son, desperate to head for the blinking, insistent lights of the far country, resorted to shocking tactics to get himself there. He staked a claim that he had no right to make while his father was still breathing. It was brash and to the point. *Show me the money.*

Commentators on the Near East all agree: the demand for an advance of the inheritance prior to his father's death was shocking, even appalling. In their view, the boy's insulting request would have been met with a stern refusal, and then he'd be driven out of the family home with verbal and perhaps even physical blows.[1] One Near Eastern scholar, writing nine hundred years ago, describes the prodigal's behavior as "despicable and childish."[2]

Another more contemporary commentator calls the request "too unthinkable to contemplate."[3] The prodigal was guilty of outrageous selfishness and sin — and that was long before he got anywhere near the far country. In verbally painting the character of the son in these darkest colors, Jesus wants us to know just how bad this boy is.

The wickedness of the young son stands in stark contrast with the glorious sunburst of love and grace that is the father in the parable. He shines long before the generosity and joy of the welcome-home barbecue. His quiet compliancy with his son's request comes as another surprise, and again is met with open-mouthed astonishment by Near Eastern writers: "The actions of the Father ... are unique, marvelous, divine actions which have not been done by any earthly father in the past."[4]

This is a love that gives us freedom to reject that very love. Salvation always remains a choice. We are invited to accept God's rescue from the consequences of sin and judgment to follow, but the offer remains an invitation; the dignity of choice is eternally ours.

The father's kindness was at great personal cost. The younger son's share of the inheritance — usually one third (with two thirds going to the older brother[5]) — was sold off quickly in a "fire" sale. Scripture says that the young son "got together all he had," which can be more literally translated as "he turned everything into cash."[6] As a result, the garage-sale pricing of this family's assets would have prompted a scandal in the wider community. How selfish and ungrateful could that upstart be, selling his own kith and kin down the river like that?

The father's behavior is certainly not as expected; a Near Eastern patriarch would not act like this. Jesus's point is not that God is like an earthly father; rather it is that God is like no earthly father that has ever been. That said, we'll see later that the father figure most likely represents Jesus: the obvious correlation between the earthly father in this story and the "Father in heaven" may not be correct. For now, suffice it to say that the son's selfishness contrasted with the father's selflessness.

At last, the hasty sell-off completed, the prodigal would have left his hometown under a cloud of terrible disgrace. It would likely be a one-way journey—and not just because of the lurking dangers of the road or the beckoning perils of the shadowy far country. Honor would ensure that he could most likely never return home. The headstrong lad had damaged his family irreparably, and the only way for him to return honorably would be as a successful businessman who had turned the cashed-out inheritance into a healthy profit to replenish the family coffers.

But there was still another shock in this part of the story to those living in the culture of the day. It is a stunning silence.

THE SOUND OF SILENCE

What Jesus *doesn't* say is shattering. Those who first heard the story would have expected it to play out something like this:

> There was a man who had two sons. The younger one said to his father, "Father, give me my share of the estate." The older son, knowing that it was his responsibility to intervene and mediate in this developing conflict came between his younger brother and his beloved father and did everything in his power to reconcile them. A peace was brokered. They all lived happily ever after. And great was the relief of the fattened calf.

Okay, so the "happily ever after" and delighted junior cow additions are the fruit of my wishful thinking, but the rest is exactly what Jesus's first hearers would have anticipated. When any conflict erupted in a Near Eastern family, a mediator would be called for. Rather than the aggrieved parties engaging in a direct, face-to-face dispute, those who were in conflict would address each other through a third party. Honor would be maintained because nobody had to directly back down, face was saved, and the negotiation would hopefully succeed. And that's where the elder brother—I like to call him big brother—would come in. Or, as in this case, he *wouldn't* come in.

In a family dispute like this, it would always be the responsibility of the oldest son in the family to act as mediator. Speaking about the big brother's role, author Kenneth Bailey describes what would have been expected:

> Middle Eastern culture has a traditional role for him that he refuses to play. As soon as his brother makes the outlandish request for his inheritance, the older son is expected to be galvanized into action. When serious breaches in relationships occur, a mediator is selected ... who is always the person with the closest relationship to both sides. The listener fully expects [the elder brother] to begin this classical and very effective process ... but rather we see an elder brother who will take and not give. He accepts the apportionment of his inheritance but will not move himself to prevent the disaster of his brother's actions ... thus all three characters are clearly delineated. The reader understands the prodigal by what he does, the father by what he gives, and the older son by what he does not do. The prodigal is on his way.[7]

Bailey, who has spent a lifetime living and studying in the Near East, much of it lovingly reflecting on the prodigal parable, describes how the cultural expectation of the eldest brother to act as mediator continues to this very day. Describing his preaching ministry in the Near East, he observes:

> In the villages ... I always ask, "Who must be the reconciler?" The villagers always answer from the pews, "His brother, of course." Everyone knows this. Furthermore, he must start immediately. It is up to him to step in at once and try and reconcile his brother to his father. The family and community demand it. But our man is silent ... *if he hated his brother, he would still fulfill this task for the sake of his father* [italics mine] ... but here the older son refuses.[8]

Big brother should have been the big peacemaker, and the fact that he did nothing is an early indictment in the parable. His kid brother became a prodigal and set out on a journey that would have been fraught with danger, and yet the older and hopefully wiser sibling didn't lift a finger to stop it from happening. Big brother does nothing to prevent a parting. The prodigal walks. Look, he fades now into the distance.

Most of us have prodigals in our lives, and how we would love to see them come home once again to God. But how much better would it be if they didn't leave in the first place? If we are to create a truly prodigal-friendly church, then we must face this challenge: Are there steps that we can take to prevent a parting?

Stop right there. Before we rush into irrational guilt, let's affirm: however dynamic, loving, and relevant the church is, some people will still walk away. We must not blame the church or ourselves for the seductive work that temptation, tragically, can accomplish in us all. Sometimes the deceptive draw of the far country seems just too luscious to resist. But as big brother failed the wayward lad, so we too will fail our prodigals if we neglect to ask searching questions of ourselves, and assume that the only journey to be made is their journey back to us. We must be willing to travel the painful road of self-examination and ask what we could have done differently. What can we do to prevent them from being so easily lured away?

WE'RE GLAD THEY LEFT ...

Perhaps the first specific question is this: do we even want them to come back? Uncomfortable though it is to admit, here is the sad news: not all churches actually want the mess, disruption, and challenge that returning prodigals (and, presumably, new converts) will invariably bring. When a conference with the theme "The Prodigal-Friendly Church" was held in the USA recently, one senior pastor wrote to express his abject disinterest in the subject. His alarming letter is amended slightly to protect the guilty.

Dear Sir,

I have received the publicity about the Prodigal-Friendly Church conference. Please take me off your mailing list. It is irrelevant to what is happening here in [town deleted] and as I see it, in most of the rest of this State. I am not going to try to bring back the prodigals. As a matter of fact, in some cases we were glad to see them go. When my wife and I came here 5 years ago, we had 35 people, so if they all came at once now, we would have to put up more chairs. We have some 90 plus people who call our church their home church ...

This man is no heartless monster; he has just settled for what any of us who are in Christian leadership can settle for: "enough" bodies in pews and dollars in the offering. As long as the "house" is full, why worry about those who have relocated? In fact, their homecoming would be an unwelcome intrusion. *More chairs needed. More dollars spent. Good riddance.*

But just as big brother was called to be a mediator, so we, the people of God, have been given the "ministry of reconciliation."[9] Surely that role of taking people by the hand and leading them to God extends beyond reaching those who have never known God's love. Our call to be reconcilers must include those who have tasted God's goodness but have been lured by forbidden fruit: the prodigals. So let's pause and ask the question: Are there factors beyond their own sin that have caused the prodigals to walk away?

WHY THEY WALKED AWAY

Some work has been done to ask the hard questions. In a recent survey, hundreds of people who had left the church in England were asked, "Why did you go?" Although every story is unique, some key reasons emerged. People abandoned the church (and sometimes God, but not necessarily) because of unfulfilled expectations, a change in personal circumstances, loss of faith, the pressure of changing values in modern culture, a lack of a sense of belonging in the church, unwillingness to commit to the cost of discipleship, and reactions to childhood upbringing.

I won't bore you with statistics and small print. Here are the headlines: The baby boomer prodigals (born between 1945 and 1960) don't like big and organized anything. Generally, they don't trust organizations and their leaders. What matters is what they feel personally, rather than being involved socially: they want the experience, but don't really want to join a club to get it. They're hungry for meaning, but often didn't find it in organized religion; many felt that attending church on a regular basis was just "going through the motions." They're consumers. Like their burgers, they want religion their way. They're impatient with mindless traditions. And those surveyed had decided that when their moral choices on issues such as drug use and sexual promiscuity conflicted with church involvement, the church had to go. In the ensuing lifestyle clash, their involvement in church was the casualty.

Baby buster prodigals (born between 1961 and 1981) have continued the quest for personal fulfillment, but they are less idealistic and more pragmatic than the boomers. At the same time, they still have a hunger to have all their senses satisfied; they too have been impatient with tradition for tradition's sake.

But the overwhelming conclusion that comes from this research is more stark: generally people who left felt that churches were often disconnected from the real world, and that they were somewhat dull too. Frequently those who have left church commented that church seemed like "another planet" or a "past culture," and that churches were failing to connect to the rest of life. Many people who drift away from church don't do so because of a cataclysmic crisis about faith or a compulsive desire to sin with vigor. Put crudely, some become so-called prodigals because they're bored stiff. And so the problem can be summarized simply: we, the people of God, can often be quite irrelevant and rather tedious. Figuratively speaking, we're playing tunes that few want to listen to, and we keep playing them over and over. If the sound is the same old thing that's been playing for decades, no wonder people are switching off.

The survey also revealed that many people became dislocated from church simply because of a change of life that disrupted their regular routine. The most frequently cited example was relocation. Habits that are disrupted by moving to a new location are not automatically taken up again. Single people, especially, may find the idea of entering a new church full of strangers too daunting. Young college students often find that their new lifestyles are not conducive to rising early on Sunday mornings. For others, the breakdown of marriage can become a barrier to attendance as they fear what others will think or say. For older people, illness can be a major factor. And so with a change in situation, habits are easily lost. But this points us to an interesting notion: Many people go to church for no other reason than that it is their habit to do so.

Their Christianity has diminished into being a dull habit, and it is one that neither comforts nor discomforts them. It's simply what they have done with their Sunday mornings, perhaps out of duty, fear, or simply because it's what they've always done: a righteous routine, a dull dirge. So when life changes, church attendance may or may not be part of the new picture. But this hardly speaks of vibrant, energetic faith and commitment. Maintaining a living faith requires imagination and an ability to dream, which fuels passion and commitment. Without that stirring, we will all settle into sleepy tedium.

In Bruce Chatwin's *The Songlines*, an Irish priest describes the connection between faith and imagination: "Flynn has to be some kind of genius ... but I don't think he was ever a believer. He could never take the leap into faith. Didn't have the imagination for it."[10]

For many prodigals, the fabulous invitation to live for the kingdom of heaven and partner with the dynamic, loving God in his purposes for humanity, has become like an endless black-and-white television miniseries. It's continuously rerun, provoking little more than a yawn. Not much to stir the imagination there.

And so some of the prodigals wander because they wonder how it is that this gospel news, touted as the most breathtaking, planet-shaking story in the history of civilization, has now become so tamed and predictable, apparently a homely message of weekly instruction for nice people who are on their way to a better (and hopefully, mildly more interesting) afterlife. For them, the "old, old story" of the gospel has indeed gotten old: they are bored believers who have tragically lost the gift of astonishment. For them, grace simply isn't so amazing anymore. In some cases, the sermon has become something that Christians endure weekly rather than eagerly anticipate. It rarely evokes the nervousness that one should feel around the ticking time bomb that is Truth. Our lives can be wonderfully disturbed when we are exposed to God's Word, shared with the thoughtful creativity that should characterize the ones who claim to speak on behalf of the Creator. But for the prodigals, all this is predictable scenery. When the worship leader insists during the Sunday morning service that heaven will be just like this, they despair at the thought of just another ten minutes, never mind an eternity. The prospect of a more-of-the-same forever looks bleak.

Of course, there's nothing wrong with the *message* of the gospel. The good news is the rock-solid foundation that is so urgently needed in a postmodern culture where the story is that there is no central story. The "Big Fat Story of God," as N. T. Wright calls it, is the most epic blockbuster of all time and the wonderful, dependable constant in a shifting-sand world—"the Great Story" as C. S. Lewis puts it. When Lewis came to the conclusion of his Chronicles of Narnia, he exclaimed, "This is the end of all the stories." But for the Narnia characters, he described an ongoing, breathtaking destiny: "It was only the beginning of the real story ... Now at last they were beginning chapter one of the Great Story, which no one on earth has read: which goes on forever: in which every chapter is better than the one before."[11]

And part of its glory is that it is the trustworthy story of the eternal God. Lloyd C. Douglas, who wrote the novel *The Robe*, tells of a retired music teacher whom he met while in university. They lived in the same lodgings, the older man disabled and unable to leave his apartment. A daily ritual of sorts developed between them. Every morning Douglas would open the old man's door and ask the same question: "Well, what's the good news?" The older gentleman would pick up his tuning fork, tap it on the metal arm of his wheelchair, and say, "That's middle C! It was middle C yesterday; it will be middle C tomorrow; it will be middle C a thousand years from now. The tenor upstairs sings flat, the piano across the hall is out of tune, but that, my friend, is middle C!"[12] God is the "middle C" of the universe, the magnificent, faithful Holy One. Our attempts to airbrush or revise him should come to nothing. The music of grace means nothing unless he is the primary chord.

The problem is not with our message, but with our methodology. Does our preaching stimulate, irritate, confront, and occasionally infuriate? Does it just take up time on Sundays, or does it drive us back to our Bibles on Mondays, eager — even desperate — to slake the wholesome thirst that has been created by a sermon? Preaching should activate an ongoing search, not end it.

Is it possible that in some of our dumbing-down of the message, we have alienated so many that they have gone away not so much in pursuit of sensuality, but on the hunt for creative and intellectual stimulation? Church gatherings that coldly dispense orthodox information without color or creativity will invariably create prodigals. In the film *Mr. Holland's Opus*, Mr. Holland tries to convince a hesitant clarinetist she is missing the point of everything: "There's a lot more to music than notes on a page. It's about feelings, and moving people, and something beautiful and being alive and having fun."[13] Surely this is what we should aspire to: to truly move and inspire. And not only should what we do as a church be stimulating, but it must equip people to live out their faith in an increasingly bewildering world.

ALL OF LIFE IS SPIRITUAL

As I write, wars rage in Iraq and Afghanistan, North Korea's godlike chief is saber-rattling, Russia's Putin is threatening, and the old Cold War is looking increasingly frosty again. Floods are devastating parts of Britain probably because of climate change, and there is an epidemic of sexually transmitted diseases among young people. Airport security remains at an all-time high because of the daily fear of terrorism. International and interreligious relations, the environment, and sexual ethics surely top the list of some of the most pressing issues of our day.

And yet the tragic reality is that some pastors and leaders are unwilling to share the complexity of what the Bible has to say on these vital subjects, fearing that they are being political or excessively controversial if they do so. Some of them are willing, but their hands are tied — or perhaps, more specifically, their mouths are gagged. They are unable to venture into discussing what we might think of as "hot potatoes," because their congregations would revolt if they did tiptoe into those territories, or worse still, go to another church. But these issues are precisely the nagging realities that are worrying everyone sick. If we don't offer God's perspective on these terrifying problems, then we must not be surprised if some drift away from the church as they look elsewhere for sensible answers.

In 1986, Yoweri Museveni became president of Uganda when his National Resistance Army overthrew the military junta. Museveni had attended Christian youth camps during his teenage years, and while at one of the camps, had asked that an evening be devoted to prayer for nearby Tanzania, which, at the time, was engaged in a terrible civil war. He was told that this request was inappropriate: "We don't concern ourselves with things like that." Prayers were held, but they focused on the needs of the camp and the spiritual well-being of those attending the event. Museveni made a decision: Christianity apparently had nothing to say about the needs of the day, so he would look elsewhere for a guiding philosophy for real life.

Rwanda is perhaps the bloodiest example of a nation that experienced a revival of piety that was socially disconnected — with horrendous results. The tragic, bloody story of that nation is a warning to us all in the worldwide family of the church.

Rwanda was one of the most evangelized of the African countries — over 80 percent of the population claimed to be Christian in the 1990s. This had stemmed from a revival in the 1930s when widespread conviction of sin, public confession, and evangelism had spread across Uganda, South Africa, Kenya, Tanzania, Burundi, and the Congo, as well as Rwanda. A favorite saying of the day among the white missionaries was that "the ground is level at the cross."

But the teaching of the church there was narrow and pietistic; it focused on blessing, experiences, and "spiritual" concerns, and failed to teach the lordship of Christ over *all* of life. When an aircraft carrying the Rwandan president was shot down in April 1994, unprecedented violence broke out between the Hutus and the Tutsis, and an estimated one million people were butchered in the ensuing violence. The church had taught a narrow understanding of the nature of sin, which centered around private morality — lying, drinking, smoking, and adultery. There was often unquestioning and naïve support of those in power. Emmanuel Kolini, of the Shoba Diocese in Zaire, has said:

> One of the problems was lack of teaching on how the Scriptures could be applied to social and practical questions ... Some missionaries taught that politics was a dirty game and the Christian duty was to escape it.[14]

And Roger Bowen, of the Mid-Africa Ministry (formerly the Rwandan Mission), writes:

> There was a need to know how to live out Christian discipleship in the secular world ... There was little awareness of the solidarities of sin that we are embedded in as members of society ... Missionaries preached a form of pietism that encouraged withdrawal from the public life of the nation or a naïve, uncritical support of the party in power.[15]

When the preaching and teaching of the church doesn't connect with the real issues of life, life itself is at stake. The prodigal-friendly church will give permission to its teachers and preachers to tread into dangerous waters, boldly seeking to bring light and truth. And if that is to happen, we must stop making a distinction about what subjects are spiritual and what are not. Irrelevance never satisfies; surely no one ever came to church to find out what happened to the Amalekites. *Life* is spiritual. Bills. Gas prices. Impotence. Orgasms. Healthcare, at home and worldwide. Troublesome neighbors and belligerent bosses. What we love, hate, or fear. It all matters to God. And he has perspectives on it all.

IT'S JUST NOT SPIRITUAL

Britain's leading Christian magazine, *Christianity,* recently took a brave step in the introduction of a column called *Dear Maggie,* which is an advice article written by a qualified sexual psychotherapist who offers an unashamedly Christian perspective on matters that many Christians are not keen on discussing. Homosexuality, masturbation, cross-dressing, pornography, and the use of sex toys by married couples: all these have been discussed with refreshing clarity in recent months.

There has been a barrage of letters in response, many of which have complained that it is inappropriate for such things to be discussed. Of course, many have also written letters of great appreciation, grateful that Christians are at last acknowledging that they are sexual beings and that discussion of sexuality is not limited to a negative context, such as when a high profile leader falls into immorality. While there are proper contexts for teaching and discussion — I'm not advocating a sermon on sex toys for the family Communion service — we must find ways to talk about these very real and relevant issues.

Most Christians spend most of their time in the workplace. But apart from the odd remark from the pulpit admonishing people not to make personal phone calls or steal the office pencils, there has been a dearth of teaching about living for Christ in that everyday context. Yet God has something to say about it all, be it sex, work, or war. Mark Green of the London Institute of Contemporary Christianity said, "The key problem is not that we have failed to notice that *work* is significant, but rather that we have not noticed that all of life is significant to the creator and redeemer God."[16]

Simon Jones emphasizes the point, urgently calling us to rugged relevance:

> The church has got to be a place where the world and people's concerns about it are taken seriously and addressed. It is no good preaching week in, week out, about speaking in tongues, sanctification, or how to praise the Lord with the latest worship CD, if we aren't also preaching about how to be Christians at work, what God thinks and feels about the world we live in, and what kind of politics honors the King of Kings.[17]

In our preaching, our praying, our priorities, we must make sure that what we do and say genuinely connects with the real world. The worship leader who says, "Let's forget the world this morning and just focus on God," has missed the point. We gather to affirm that there is more to life than what we see. But when we do that as pious escapism, we risk that some will plot their own escape — from church itself. The prodigal-friendly church must be a relevant church.

POWER TO THE PEOPLE

In our desperation to recruit people for ministry *within* the church, we must beware lest we devalue what most people do for the kingdom of God *outside* of the church. Mark Green puts it this way:

> We can tell what's important to a church (or any organization) by the heroes that it celebrates and the stories it tells. Are most of the church's heroes preachers and teachers,

mainly white, and mainly male? Why are you a hero if you teach a Sunday school, but not if you teach 150 Muslim, Hindu and secular kids in an inner city school Monday through Friday?[18]

One British-based congregation is trying to bridge the gap by insisting that they don't get preoccupied with "church" matters. They changed the format of their business meetings to focus on what happened *beyond* the building, rather than *inside* it. The quarterly meeting was to be a "business of the people of the church" meeting. They held a "job fair" in the church hall, open to all in the church family to attend. The fair featured, among others, realtors, policemen and women, a physiotherapist, and school teachers. All were available to talk about what they did with most of their lives. At the end of the evening, there was a time of prayer for them all. The next quarter, the focus was on what people did with their leisure time. Elected officers of school PTAs, members of soccer teams, Girl Guides and Boy Scout leaders all shared what they did. The church was greatly encouraged as its members felt heard, as they saw the breadth of their influence in their community, and as they realized that they were truly living life together in line with their stated values. Connected life is what the prodigal-friendly church does.

TRUTH AND MYSTERY

Prodigals sometimes head for the horizon because they feel that there is a famine of answers to help them navigate life's maze. But some leave because they have swallowed slogans and superficial answers that oversimplify life's complexity. We must face the uncomfortable fact that we don't have the definitive answer for everything, and that those who try to hawk quick, easy solutions will be found guilty of superficiality. If we teach a theology of healing, then we must also follow that up with a theology of suffering — one that goes beyond the crushing, thoughtless indictment, "Well, you just didn't have enough faith."

The ability to confess that we do not know everything is wonderfully liberating. It acknowledges that there is One who *does* know, and that one day we shall have greater understanding in the clearer air and bluer sky of eternity, but that in the meantime, mysteries remain. This is part of the essence of true faith rather than a flimsy façade of faith. Consequently, we must release people to not know, lest would-be prodigals run out of church when they run out of answers. Reinhold Niebuhr said, "Nothing which is true or beautiful or good makes complete sense in any immediate context of history; therefore we must be saved by faith."[19]

Faith is not about understanding everything. Loralee Hagan confesses, "I cannot completely believe in a God that I can understand completely."[20] Faith is surely the acknowledgement that, through God's revelation, we do know something about everything, but we don't yet know everything about everything. To offer anything else will surely disappoint, and lead us into arrogant self-deception. We remain human; God remains God.

C. S. Lewis's *The Horse and His Boy* is the story of a boy, Shasta, and his horse, Bree. They are joined by another rider, Aravis, and her horse, Hwin. Bree scoffs at Aravis's description of Aslan, the great deliverer of Narnia. Aravis thinks that Aslan might actually be a real lion. In his mocking, Bree doesn't notice that Hwin and Aravis are staring wide-eyed at something on the wall behind him:

> While Bree spoke they saw an enormous lion leap up from the outside and balance itself onto the green wall; only it was a brighter yellow and it was bigger and more beautiful and more alarming than any lion they had ever seen. And at once it jumped down inside the wall and began approaching Bree from behind. It made no noise at all. And Hwin and Aravis couldn't make any noise themselves, no more than if they were frozen.
>
> "No doubt," continued Bree, "when they speak of him as a Lion they only mean he is as strong as a lion or (to our enemies, of course) as fierce as a lion. Or something of that kind. Even a little girl like you, Aravis, must see it

would be quite absurd to suppose he is a *real* lion. Indeed it would be disrespectful. If he was a lion he would have to be a Beast just like the rest of us. Why!" (and here Bree began to laugh) "if he was a lion he would have four paws, and a tail and *Whiskers!* ... Aie, ooh, hoo-hoo! Help!"

For just as he said the word *Whiskers* one of Aslan's had actually tickled his ear. Bree shot away like an arrow to the other side of the enclosure and there turned; the wall was too high for him to jump and he could fly no farther. Aravis and Hwin both started back ...

"Now Bree," [Aslan] said, "you poor, proud, frightened Horse, draw near. Nearer still, my son. Do not dare not to dare. Touch me. Smell me. Here are my paws, here is my tail, these are my whiskers. I am a true Beast."

"Aslan," said Bree in a shaken voice, "I'm afraid I must be rather a fool."

"Happy the Horse who knows that while he is still young. Or the Human either."[21]

Truth and mystery: these must coexist in the prodigal-friendly church.

LOST IN THE CROWD

As a Brit living in America, I have tried to gain understanding about some of the sports so beloved here, such as baseball and football. As a result, I have enjoyed the experience of cheering a gaggle of crash-helmeted, shoulder-padded youths as they dash around a field and seem to take much pleasure in physically assaulting each other. And, living near Denver, I have witnessed quite a number of Colorado Rockies games. But I have a confession to make: I don't understand either game at all. I can't fathom why it is that, in football, a chap pops up to measure the field so frequently, and the obsession with statistics that afflicts baseball (speed of pitch, batting average, number of times batter scratched his head) baffles and bewilders me. So now I don't watch the games. Instead I watch the crowd, I eat a hot dog or three, and I at times even enter into the corporate excitement when "my" team does something clever. I rise to my feet, cheer very loudly, and feel rather pleased if they win. But to tell the truth, I really don't have the first clue about what's going on.

I fear something similar can happen in our churches, especially our stronger, more dynamic churches. It's possible to attend a great church, cheer when prompted, enjoy the experience, feel a part of the event — and yet have no foundational understanding of what Christianity is all about. We feel exhilarated as we breathe in the collective ether of the church. We become preoccupied with its vision and even busy with its activities. And yet at the heart of the excitement and activity, there is hollowness because we neglect to put down our own roots. And then when personal trouble arrives, or the church hits a difficult and more barren patch (as all churches will do), then we find ourselves high and dry. Surely many people drift away from faith because they were never properly grounded in faith in the first place.

When we consider how the Christian church, especially in the first four centuries, developed a process for "sound conversion," we must be challenged by their rigorous plan and commitment to ground new believers in their Christian lives. The early church gave themselves to the training of new believers, a practice they called the *catechumenate*, derived from the Greek word *katechein*, meaning "to teach" or "instruct." Becoming fully integrated into the life of the church community was a lengthy process. It is often taught that the early church immediately baptized their converts and so we should do likewise, but this practice ceased fairly quickly. So why the shift away from the early apostolic practice of baptizing immediately after profession of faith to delaying baptism until after substantive training and mentoring?

The change came because leaders were concerned about "the sincerity of the conversion of the candidates."[22] By the second century, the church developed a lengthy catechumenate, which was required training for all who requested baptism. Those who led these catechumenate groups had a deep love for the people in their care; St. Augustine advised his friend Deogratias about how to carry out his teaching responsibilities with the catechumens. "We should endeavor to meet them with a brother's, a father's, and a mother's love," and seek to be "united with them thus in heart."[23]

Great efforts were made to help new Christians put down deep roots. They took their time, usually over a three-year span,[24] and some of the best-known church leaders of the first four centuries were devoted to teaching new believers. Origen (185–254), a great scholar, had a passionate concern for training new believers in the Scriptures and grounding them in the faith; he was a very popular teacher.

The catechumens knew what they believed. Vast portions of Scripture were read, and teachers would also provide *explanations* of Scripture. The *Apostolic Tradition* reveals that, in some places, the catechumens gathered together early in the morning, before going to work, for Scripture reading, teaching, and prayer.[25] New converts understood the "big story" of God. In his work on catechizing, Augustine strongly emphasized that it is vital for the teacher to lay out the broad sweep of salvation history. Both creeds and Scripture were prioritized for these catechumens prior to baptism: truth received and truth corporately declared.

If we are to prevent a prodigal's parting, we must take seriously the need to provide grounding for Christians so that their faith will not evaporate with the first hint of a challenge. At Timberline Church, the influx of brand-new Christians and returning prodigals caused Dary Northrop to consider his preaching very seriously. He'd always sought to teach with accessibility and clarity so that the sermon would inspire and equip, but as he looked into the eyes of these new people, many of them battling addictions, he faced a fresh challenge:

> I had to ask myself—what can I give them that will help them get through tomorrow? What we were talking about in church didn't work for them, didn't matter to them.

We had to talk about stuff that was new to us, we had to develop programs and ministries that would meet these needs. We had to do it. Ministers sometimes hardly ever talk to people outside of their churches, and so they don't know what the real issues are. We had to face those issues head on — and respond to them.

As we allow ourselves to be challenged about boring, irrelevant, disconnected church that doesn't foundationally equip people for life in the real world, we must do the hard work to prevent a parting.

NO FOND FAREWELL

It would have been a very difficult, tense few days. Everyone in the family would have known what was going on as the sell-off took place in the community. Finally, it was time for the young lad to leave for the road stretching to the horizon of the far country.

Perhaps big brother came into the house and noticed that his father's eyes were red, his cheeks still showing traces of tears. Perhaps he ran to the door and could see his young brother, now a distant, fading figure. There's still time. Desperate though the situation is, he could still intervene. Yell. Jump up and down, and wave his arms. *Come back. Let's talk this through. There is another way.*

But none of this happens. Big brother turns, shrugs his shoulders, and heads off in the opposite direction, back to the fields, back to work. Back to business as usual.

Perhaps we can do better. As we continue to wrestle with tough questions ourselves, I hope that many would-be prodigals find ample reason to cancel their farewells altogether.

Chapter 5

SERENADE: AN UNCOMMON HOMECOMING

Serenade: A lighthearted piece, written in several movements, usually as background music for a social function.

When he came to his senses, he said, "How many of my father's hired men have food to spare, and here I am starving to death! I will set out and go back to my father and say to him: Father, I have sinned against heaven and against you. I am no longer worthy to be called your son; make me like one of your hired men." So he got up and went to his father.

But while he was still a long way off, his father saw him and was filled with compassion for him; he ran to his son, threw his arms around him and kissed him.

The son said to him, "Father, I have sinned against heaven and against you. I am no longer worthy to be called your son."

But the father said to his servants, "Quick! Bring the best robe and put it on him. Put a ring on his finger and sandals on his feet. Bring the fattened calf and kill it. Let's have a feast and celebrate. For this son of mine was dead and is alive again; he was lost and is found." So they began to celebrate.

LUKE 15:17–24

It was a chilling ceremony carefully designed to strike terror to the heart. Its name says it all. *Kezazeh.* The Aramaic word is translated "cutting off." *Kezazeh* was a simple but devastating ritual that was like a funeral for one not yet dead, so terrible and final was it. It solemnized the total rejection and alienation of one who had fallen afoul of the community.

You're nothing.

Banished.

Unwelcome here.

Be gone for good.

And let others be warned: this could happen to you too.

Kezazeh would be enacted for a variety of reasons. The victim might suffer it because he had sold property to a Gentile.[1] But more specifically, if a Jewish boy lost his inheritance among the Gentile population and attempted to return home, *kezazeh* would begin. As he approached his town or village, a hostile group would come towards him. News travels fast in tight-knit Eastern communities, so a person who unexpectedly appeared on the horizon would be identified quickly, and, if he was deemed guilty and unwelcome, he'd be intercepted before he reached his home. Then the awful ceremony would start, the beginning of the end.

The angry-faced villagers would place parched corn and nuts into a jar, and then smash it to pieces, crying out the name of the despised one, announcing that, from that moment on, he was totally cut off from the community. The shards of clay were strewn across the sand, never to be joined again, so the symbolism was obvious: Our relationship is irretrievably shattered. *Kezazeh* was no idle threat. Even today, Near Eastern village culture is ruthless with anyone who has failed. Beggars are at the mercy of everyone's taunting; even children join in with the tirades. Little wonder that one rabbi warns, "Slander by the whole town is a terror worse than death."[2]

When Jesus spoke of the prodigal son returning home, the crowd who first heard the great story would have leaned forward in anticipation. Most likely they anticipated what would come next: the trauma of *kezazeh*. Anything less was impossible. As we've seen, there was only one way for the prodigal to escape this judgment: he would have to return from his trip a triumphant businessman, bringing a healthy profit with him. The cash he'd made could then be used to repurchase the land that had been so hastily sold off. All would be forgiven.

But he's lost all the money. And not only that, he's squandered it in Gentile country. He's been slumming it with pigs, the animals most despised in the culture. For Jesus's audience, it didn't get much worse than that.

There was only one other slim hope for the prodigal; there was the faintest chance that he might be able to work off his debt. Even though it would take years, it would be worth it in the end. That's why the returning prodigal came asking for work, not son-ship. The decades of repayment would be hard, but at least, the lad figured, he would be able to eat. His father's servants had food to spare. He would survive.

And yet his proposal would only work if he escaped the awful ceremony. He might never get the chance to plead with his father if he was sent packing by those angry and anxious for justice, for the eagle-eyed villagers watched and waited, ready to gather and hurl their verbal stones. *Break the jar, break his heart.*

But someone else was also watching, someone who had been planning another community-wide gathering. It was the father—and he was a party planner.

A STUNNING WELCOME

Perhaps the lad saw the distant figure racing towards him and braced himself for what was to come. This was surely the first of many villagers. In minutes they would gather, summoned by the blood-curdling yells that announced that he was approaching the village, excited with the cruel passion that humans often enjoy as they gloat over the downfall of another. Sure enough, one or two others now joined the man who was moving fast towards him. Here they come.

But then the lad focused on the faces of those men closing in on him.

Did he think that it was the result of too many hours trudging through the sand in the punishing sun? Had his terrible lifestyle and hideous diet weakened his brain as well as his body? Were his eyes playing tricks on him? Because the man ...

... looked like his father. And the men with him, frantically trying to keep up with their boss, were his servants. No *kezazeh* crowd today. Bewilderingly, it really *was* his father. Running.

The sight of a sprinting parent is no surprise in our culture: not so in Jesus's day. Near Eastern gentlemen didn't run in public—and they still don't. One rabbi, writing about two hundred years before Christ, expresses how a slow-paced walk was synonymous with dignity. "A man's manner of walking tells you what he is."[3] And it was not just dignity that made a man walk slowly—practicality prevented him from running. Men wore long robes that covered the feet, and so in order to run, one had to hoist the robes up, exposing the legs, which was considered a shameful and humiliating act. Priests offering sacrifices were not even allowed to lift their robes to avoid the pools of blood that inevitably formed. Also, popular teaching dictated that if a bird got under the hem of a man's robe on the Sabbath, he was prohibited from lifting it—the bird had to stay there until sunset. When an Old Testament prophet sought for words to describe the utter humiliation of God's people, he used the imagery of bare legs to portray their shame:

Tie up your robe
Uncover your legs
Pass through the rivers
Your nakedness shall be uncovered
And your shame will be seen[4]

For Near Eastern biblical scholars, the imagery of a father running was too shocking; hence the Arabic translation of the prodigal story omits the picture of the running father. It simply states that he "went" to the son. For a thousand years, Near Eastern Bible translators used other phrases, affronted by the ungainly portrait of a father, skirts in hand, hotfooting it towards his scarecrow son. The notion of this respected gentleman — a man of considerable means with his servants, fattened calves, and other chattels of wealth — *sprinting* was just too unpalatable to Near Eastern sensibilities. To make matters "worse," the father ran in broad daylight, which we know because he was able to see his son while he was still a distance away.

The father tossed his dignity and self-respect to one side, for the only thing that mattered was that his lovely boy was home. As I mentioned earlier, the running father figure in the story most likely represents Jesus. The three portraits of the woman, the shepherd, and now the sprinting father in this parable are all images of one who goes *out* on a search-and-rescue mission. While the prodigal was *still a long way off* he was met by love that came running. This is surely a portrait of incarnation and of the glorious truths celebrated by Paul when he wrote in Romans, "But God demonstrates his own love for us in this: While we were still sinners, Christ died for us,"[5] and in Ephesians, "He came and preached peace to you who were far away and peace to those who were near."[6]

Don't forget why Jesus told the story. He was being criticized and was therefore defending his behavior, especially his choice of dinner companions. Now the father figure slams into his son in a collision of love.

The details of the wonderful reunion are well known. Jesus describes a dad who *kept on* kissing his son. Far more than polite pecks, in that culture these kisses signify forgiveness, peace, and love — a symbol of reconciliation.

The best robe — one that belonged to the father — was hurriedly placed on the prodigal's shoulders even before he had a chance to clean up. The father would have been anxious that the arriving villagers would not see his son's threadbare, filthy rags, and with the urgent command, "Quick," hastens to cover his shame. Seeing the parental robe, the villagers would know immediately that they were not even to think about beginning *that* ceremony.

This is my son, you know, the father was saying to them all. Hence the running and the urgent commands.

A ring, most likely a signet ring,[7] was hastily placed on his bony finger. This was the seal used to stamp legal documents, including wills, which is remarkable when we consider the prodigal's track record of squandering the family assets. The one who has been so reckless is trusted immediately.

Shoes were placed on his feet, a simple but profound symbol. Slaves go barefoot; only sons wear shoes in the family home. Dignity demanded that shoes be worn, for to be without them invited derision. In the Talmud, a Sadducee notices a rabbi without shoes and insults him by saying, "He who rides on a horse is a king, upon an ass, is a free man, and he who has shoes on his feet is a human being, but he who has none of these, one who is dead and buried is better off." No wonder the Jews have a saying: "One should sell even the beams of his house and buy shoes for his feet."

To go barefoot was also a sign of penitence ("Take off your shoes, this is holy ground"[8]). By having sandals placed upon the filthy feet of the prodigal, the father was making an eloquent statement. *Wipe your tears away. Cancel your "make me a servant" speech. You can only enter the family home once again as a fully restored son.*

The *kezazeh* ritual was cancelled, and in its place was a generous, expressive, shocking, layers-of-love welcome. We are called to offer the same warm hug and kiss today. Sadly, the church is not always thought of as the place with the best party in town. A leader laments:

> A friend of mine leads a church in Wales. Noticing real problems of teenage pregnancy, drug abuse, and prostitution in their town, they decided to set up a project to offer support and life-skills training to the young girls caught in this cycle. Over time a group of these young mums became interested in the wider life of the church and the message of Christianity—some of them just could not

understand why people were so ready to serve and support them without any payment or reward. The week before Mother's Day, one of the project workers invited them to the special Sunday morning Mother's Day service. Almost all of the girls expressed an interest in coming along, but seemed slightly nervous. Eventually one of them plucked up the courage to raise the question that the rest of the group had been silently thinking, but didn't have the confidence to verbalize. "Does your church have a side door?" she asked. The project worker was surprised. After hesitating, she explained that it did, but wondered to herself about the relevance of the building's architecture. "Well," the girl explained, "people like us aren't really the sort you want marching through the front door — proud as anything. We'll come, but we'd feel a lot better if we can come in through the side door so that nobody will notice us."[9]

WELCOME TO ALL

The church is called to welcome absolutely everyone. No side doors. Period. That welcome is to be extended regardless of a person's creed, sexuality, political affiliation, and past or present sins. Welcome is not an option, but is the absolute bottom line for any congregation that wishes to legitimately describe itself in biblical terms as a church. Grace means that the red carpet should be rolled out for everyone, because we are a people who exist for all, whoever they are, and wherever they've been.

I've racked my brain and have wondered if I should bring some words of qualification to this exhortation that we welcome all. The only hesitation I have is the delicate issue of how to handle pedophiles in the church. I mention this here because I know of a church that felt that an unreserved welcome for all meant that a man who was specifically targeting churches (children are probably more accessible in churches than anywhere else) was allowed to do his dreadful work unchallenged. It's worth saying that the pedophile must find a welcome among God's people: pedophiles are the new lepers in our culture, the social equivalent of the tax gatherers who were viewed as beyond redemption—which of course they are not. But sensible precautions must be taken to disciple them in open, healthy small-group settings and to restrict easy access to children. With that sensible qualification (and one that is vital, because our welcome of children also means that we protect them from predators), I want to say that the church is called to welcome all, for we are, as Archbishop William Temple famously quipped, "the only organization on earth that exists for the benefit of its non-members." Put succinctly, we the church are created for *others*.

Chick Yuill has served in the Salvation Army for many years. He describes the inclusive passion that burned in the hearts of the Army's founders:

William Booth was a man in desperate need of inspiration. And he needed it quickly. Someone had come up with the bright idea that he should send a telegram around the world, something to stir up the troops and enthuse them for the challenges and trials that lay ahead. The question was, what should he say? The blank sheet of paper lay frustratingly on the desk in front of him; and the eager assistant, whose task it was to deliver the message to the telegraph office, stood impatiently in the doorway behind him.

But Booth was a past master of the bon mot—the right word for the right moment. One word that would be understood in every culture, one word that would remind his soldiers of their commitment to serve and of the constituency that depended on them; and—no small consideration for a man who had learned that every penny had to be raised and spent carefully—one word that would minimise the cost of the telegram. So once again he took up his pen, this time to write a word of only six letters—o-t-h-e-r-s. The job was done, the impatient messenger was despatched, and a challenge had been sounded which confronts not only Booth's Army but the whole church to this very day.[10]

If we are to respond to that challenge to center ourselves around others, then a radical, inclusive welcome is needed. Yuill goes on to call the church to that costly rolling out of the red carpet:

[We must] re-examine our attitudes to those whose life-styles, particularly in the area of sexual morality, fall short of accepted Christian standards. If we are to be the inclusive church, how are we to react to gay and lesbian couples, or cohabiting heterosexual couples who seek fellowship with us? Accepting people does not, of course, mean endorsing their way of life; but nor should it mean keeping them at arm's length until they have come up to the standard we ask. The church, we must always remember, is full of very imperfect followers of Jesus. For all of my lifetime, churches have been able to accommodate people whose unwillingness to tithe and give generously has indicated their greed, people whose more than ample girth has revealed their tendency to gluttony, and people whose wagging tongues have announced that they have fallen prey to the sin of gossip. Why then should it be any different for those who are gay or whose sins are just a little more public than my private failings? Jesus' invitation to come and follow was made to twelve very imperfect men who failed him and ran away at his hour of greatest need. We must allow God to be God as we make that same invitation today to equally imperfect people, irrespective of their social standing, their racial or ethnic origins, their sexual orientation, their past failures, or their present moral and spiritual shortcomings. Jesus himself said that his purpose in coming to earth was not to call the righteous but to be the friend of all kinds of sinners. In living out that purpose, he demonstrated his Father's heart, spending his days and giving his life for the sake of others without distinction. If we are genuinely to live for others it will mean nothing less than his life lived over again in each of us and in all of our churches, nothing less than allowing God to be God in us. It will probably mean that just about everything we have held dear will change radically and for ever. It will certainly cost us everything, but it will be the best bargain we ever made.[11]

The prodigal-friendly church will be a place of unreserved welcome, a theme that we shall continue to explore as we continue our journey through this book together.

What's that? I hear someone protest, "This sumptuous welcome was only given to the prodigal when he came home in repentance to the father's house. When people come with remorse, genuinely wanting to change, *then* we'll welcome them, but not until."

But is that *really* what the story says?

A FLAWED HOMECOMING

I've preached it myself. The famous line from the story, translated in the NIV as "when he came to his senses" and elsewhere as "when he came to himself," has launched a thousand sermons about the prodigal finally "seeing the light" when he was in dire straits in the far country. I've even preached that any reunion was impossible before this happened, citing the fact that the father did not go looking for the son when he was away (and, stunningly, I ignored the father running out to his son as well as the two episodes of the searching shepherd and the coin-hunting woman in the process!). Some seem to interpret this to mean that hugs can be offered, but they are only offered to those, like the prodigal, who have seen the error of their ways. But a closer look at the story demonstrates that the prodigal's homecoming wasn't quite the repentant act that I'd originally envisaged.

When we read that the young lad "came to himself," some say that this means precisely that—he came back to his own resources, his own ideas, or, as one Arabic translator puts it, "He got smart." Others translate this as "he took an interest in himself." Without getting into linguistic technicalities, there's a strong argument for the possibility that, rather than turning to God, he turned to himself and, in fact, came up with a proposal that his father completely ignored. It seems that the prodigal might have still been looking out for number one when he headed home. For over eighteen hundred years, some Near Eastern translations of this story (Arabic and Syriac) include no hint that the prodigal was repentant.

Check his motives. He did not come to an overwhelming sense of shame about the pain that he had brought upon his father and family, and the loss suffered by them because of his selfishness. Rather than a crisis of conscience, it's the rumbling of an empty stomach that he feels most intensely. He realizes that home is better, because home is where food is in plentiful supply. He heads home because he's starving, not because he's remorseful.

Finally, there's an interesting piece of background information to the words that Jesus the storyteller put in the prodigal's mouth. When the prodigal declares, "I have sinned against heaven and against you," he directly quoted some very well-known words, spoken in Old Testament times by a man who was *faking* repentance, trying to manipulate his way out of a tight spot. Pharaoh, bewildered by the assortment of plagues that were hitting Egypt, used this very same phrase in a conniving speech to Moses.[12] Jesus told this story to a crowd that would have included some highly accomplished theologians and historians, and in the Aramaic version of the story, the quote from Pharaoh is exact, word for word. It's likely that they would have made the connection. Is it possible that Jesus was hinting that the prodigal's heart was not quite as smitten with genuine remorse as we might at first think?

And the "make me a hired servant" proposal has about it the sense that, while the prodigal was not worthy of being called a son *now*, in the *future* he could earn his way back into worthiness again.

At very best—and giving the prodigal considerable benefit of the doubt—his repentance was imperfect (isn't it always?). He came home in a mess that was not just about his hygiene or the state of his clothing. But he still received a wonderful welcome.

The prodigal-friendly church welcomes the still-in-process prodigals because that's all each one of us is this side of eternity. Yes, God has saved us, changed us, made us to be what we were not. And yet we too continue with the faint or putrid whiff of sin about us, we who have been shown great grace are called to continue to pass grace on, to whoever needs it.

And that even includes a murderer like Saul ...

Chapter 6

INTERMEZZO: THE VERY BEST FOR THE WORST OF SINNERS

Intermezzo: A short movement or interlude connecting the main parts of the composition.

Imagine this. You're a rookie Christian of some three years standing. Your life has been utterly turned right-side up by a stunning supernatural encounter with Jesus. All that you once held dear no longer sparkles, especially your former religious confidence, which you had clung to as the number one priority of your life. Not now. Arrogant, self-righteous religion always ends up in the dumpster when we truly encounter Jesus.

Your newfound faith has cost you dearly. You've lost everything: like-minded friends, that golden-boy career, financial security, and the place of respect and honor in the community. Once you were a power broker, a Mr. Big whose word was usually a command. You've been used to being at the top of the class, the one who had his photo in the yearbook under the heading *most likely to succeed*. Now you're nothing; when it comes to your place in the pecking order, you've plummeted. You've felt the lonely draft of one who dares to step outside of a rigidly zealous community where everyone passionately believes the same thing. Once the darling of them all, now you're an outcast, an object of scorn.

But it gets worse. Your recent life choices have made a few powerful people very, very angry. Now there's a price on your head. You're under constant threat from enraged fanatics who have vowed to die rather than let you live. Already you've made a narrow escape from a murderous plot by a ring of deadly assassins. Who knows when they might strike again? You lay awake at night and sweat through too many sleepless hours. In your nightmares, predictably, you're always running. And the rising sun brings no relief. Every alleyway, every shadow could be hiding your enemies. Each morning you wake with the same thought: this dawn could be your last.

And so you decide to become part of a church where you've not been before. You've heard good things about the leaders there, and you're eagerly anticipating joining the family. You're hoping for a warm welcome, some open-house hospitality, and perhaps some prayers for protection, and so you show up.

But everyone in the place flattens against the wall in fear. Horrified, you realize that the look of terror in their eyes is because of *you*. You stammer out your wonderful story, tell about what God has done for you and through you, your words tumbling, your eyes shining, hopeful. But still you get a stonewall response. They don't believe a single word of it. Paralyzed by fear, they're convinced that you're bogus, an old enemy gone undercover. They want nothing to do with you.

So what now? Your former friends are now your enemies, and these people who should be your new family are counting you as an enemy too. Not encouraging.

All of this happened when arch-persecutor of Christians Saul became Paul. Okay, his story is an extreme example. This was the man who had spearheaded the persecution against the Jerusalem-based Christians with a systematic, obsessive campaign of terror that began with the stoning of Stephen.[1] Enflamed with a passion to shed as much Christian blood as possible, Saul had become a fearsome figurehead. Women as well as men were dragged off to prison, where many died. Others were tortured and beaten, with only one way out: Saul wanted them to blaspheme their Christ. Armed with the authority of the chief priests of the city, he continued his rampage far and wide, even pressing his campaign in foreign places.[2]

So perhaps Saul shouldn't have been so surprised when he showed up at the church at Jerusalem announcing a change of name and, more importantly, a change of heart. The fear-fuelled cold shoulder that he received was understandable. Surely some of the members of this church had lost loved ones during the terrible years when Saul had been at his heartless worst. Perhaps some of them remembered sobbing children clutching fathers as they were hauled away, or women screaming in terror as they were bundled off into the dark night. Perhaps some children grew up with only memories of Mom and Dad, all victims of Saul's voracious appetite for brutality done in the name of God.

How they hated Saul—and for very good reason. He was like a concentration camp guard to a Jew; like a Robin Island torturer to a black South African from the terrible apartheid years. By his own admission, Saul had served on many juries when the vote—for death or clemency—was cast against Christians. He had given countless believers the thumbs down.[3] And now he received a congregation-wide thumbs down himself.

Not wanted here. Thanks, but no thanks.

Then a man with an open, friendly face stepped up. His name was Barnabas, a name that means "son of encouragement," and he lived up to it wonderfully.

Take my hand, Saul. I'll stand with you and stake my reputation on you.

Barnabas takes Saul to the brothers and they extend "the right hand of fellowship" to him, a quaint saying that speaks of welcome, acceptance, favor, and trust. In ancient times, the handshake had a deeper significance than a deal done; it spoke of trustworthiness and partnership—"fellowship," as Paul put it when he wrote later to the Galatians.[4] Freeze the frame and see the welcoming, prodigal-friendly church in action.

You see, it's not just about having the right music, the snazziest program, and a seventeen-step campaign to bring prodigals rushing back at speed. Being prodigal-friendly is about creating a *culture* of welcome, rather than just appointing a welcome team. It's about becoming a people who decide that risky welcome is not someone else's job or responsibility—it's mine. It's about breaking away from the warm comfortable chat on a Sunday morning with friends, or that conversation that you've eagerly anticipated all week and meandering over to that person who seems a little alone and lost.

And, of course, it's much more than that. Every time a new person becomes part of a church, that church takes on a new responsibility. There's another mouth, spiritually speaking, to feed. Another influence on the way that things are. Who knows, they may end up actually helping lead the outfit. Saul, as we all know, became Paul and changed the history of the church and the world.

Of course, none of this would have happened if it hadn't been for Barnabas's brave kindness that prompted a handshake — at last — from the other Jerusalem leaders. Because of Barnabas's initiative, Saul was changed forever.

Such acts of transformational kindness happen day after day. Let me share just one, for Ken, like Saul, was another tough guy changed for eternity. And all it took for him was a brief meeting with Marge.

WARM MARGE AND COLD KEN

Ken was the kind of man who bought his clothes at the Big & Tall store, and he certainly had the imposing attitude to match his imposing size. As a result, he had been told that he was so nasty, so wicked, that the only thing left for him to do was to go to a church. He chose Timberline, and so now he stood in the back row of pews, his cold, dark eyes staring, unblinking, straight ahead, his body a solid, stiff mass of muscle. He was contained, angry, desperate to be switched off by this experience of church. He hadn't survived the terrible events of his life to date by being openhearted or sensitive. He was going to get through this service and then get out, having proven to himself that there was no God, or at least, no God who would be interested in him, and that his feeling of indifference was mutual. All he had to do was concentrate on not being affected by the music, the sermon, the smiles.

But he hadn't reckoned on Marge. An elderly lady, with silver hair and a sunny smile, she walked up to Ken and looked up—quite a way up, in fact, for he was about three feet taller than her. Unperturbed, she grinned broadly. Tight-lipped, he said nothing. *Concentrate. Don't waver.*

"I don't believe we've met," said Marge kindly. She was surprised to find Ken collapsing in tears on her shoulder and suddenly sobbing his way out of the wasted years, the brutality, the addictions, the life-is-cheap-just-give-me-cash years.

Marge was momentarily alarmed. "I'm sorry, was it something I said?" she inquired, genuinely concerned. Later that morning Ken got himself the beginnings of a new life.

Marge, it *was* something you said, and something you did. Something so simple, so easy, so wonderfully devastating. You were like that hotfooting dad who dashed to his son and devastated him with little more than a hug. You were like Barnabas, who threw caution to the wind and took a chance on Saul.

You shared a warm word of welcome. Perhaps you were a little nervous, walking up to that giant of a man. That boldness of yours might have taken you out of your comfort zone. But for Ken, that's all it took.

Chapter 7

SUBITO: THE SUDDEN RETURN OF THE "GOOD GUY"

Subito: Suddenly.

Meanwhile, the older son was in the field ...
LUKE 15:25 (EMPHASIS ADDED)

He was always thought of as the sensible one. Mature, reliable, and trustworthy, he was a striking contrast to the black sheep of the family—his kid brother. No slacker, the older brother worked long days in the shimmering fields. He was the stay-at-home son. The unremitting, blinking lights of the far country had failed to catch his eye or seduce his heart; he was far too sensible. The wider community would have seen him as his father's consolation; heartbroken as the old man would have been over the loss of his younger son, at least he still had his firstborn at home. And *that* lad wasn't likely to get itchy feet and go wandering. Solid as a rock, he followed the rules and obeyed his father's orders. He was a good guy. But by suddenly disrupting the party in full swing, he was utterly and totally in the wrong.

And so, at times, are we.

THE "GOOD" GUYS

Radical.

It's a word that we Christians often use to describe the nature of our faith. We talk about *radical* discipleship, *radical* commitment, and *radical* obedience. *Radical* is a word often used by think-out-of-the-box progressive church-planters who are weary of what the church has become and are experimenting with new ways to build effective kingdom communities.

It's a pertinent word to describe the true nature of the Christian life. We stand in the noble, bloodied line of many who have died rather than deny Christ—true radicals. The battle rages still. Around the world, more Christians are becoming martyrs today than during the terrible persecutions of the first century. The call of Jesus is a radical call; he comes as no add-on, no mere religious extension to our lives or a weekend hobby. He invites us to give him all of ourselves. That's radical.

I know of one radical group in particular who were working tirelessly to see their towns and cities transformed. They have lived the ultimate "purpose-driven lives," with an unwavering passion to see an end to the corruption, oppression, and darkness that shrouds their nation. Convinced that God is the only answer to the needs of messed-up humanity, they have longed to see a spiritual revival that will result in the masses bowing the knee in obedience to God's will. Their commitment to diligently study Scripture impresses. No mere armchair theorists, much of their everyday conversation is about practical theology; they've longed to end all divisions between the sacred and the secular, and have taught that the whole of life should be lived before God. For them, every moment matters. The sweat and toil of all work is worship, as is every meal they eat. Determined reformers, they've long insisted that God's presence is not limited to special buildings, but that he is to be worshiped everywhere. They've gathered frequently for conferences where gifted speakers teach. Personal spirituality is a top priority: most of this group prays for around three hours daily. For decades they have looked expectantly for the Messiah's coming, and have busied themselves in teaching about the judgment to come. Their theology includes a belief that the supernatural power of God is unleashed in his world, and they have been convinced that we are all engaged in a drama that involves players mostly unseen by the human eye, where angels and demons silently skirmish. They are committed to peace and nonviolence. They are a lay movement and believe that God has purposes for all who know him.

Are we impressed, perhaps even intimidated by them yet? This group embodies zeal, discipline, and radicalism. Personal holiness matters greatly. *Compromise* is a dirty word. They look and sound quite like us.

They were called the Pharisees. Some of them were among those muttering men on the edge of the crowd that were so bitterly critical. They endlessly frustrated Jesus. They dogged his footsteps, posed tripwire questions for him, schemed, and accused him at every turn. They tagged him as a child of Satan[1] and helped to steer him to his death. And the saddest irony is this: they too were good people gone wrong.

MISGUIDED PASSION

There were several thousand Pharisees in Jesus's day, spread throughout Israel.[2] They longed for their country's political liberation and to see the nation purged of paganism. The Jewish historian Philo, a contemporary of Jesus and Paul, describes the Pharisees as "full of zeal for the laws, the strictest guardians of the ancestral traditions."[3] Like the scribes, who were closely associated with the Pharisees (especially in Matthew's gospel), they were experts in the legalities of religion. The scribes were fascinated by what we might call Law trivia, examining every word in microscopic detail and formulating complex principles around the 248 positive and 365 negative commands of the Pentateuch, the first five books of the Bible.

But sometimes "experts" make a big mess. The scribes and the Pharisees created a bewildering religious maze, overwhelming in its complexity, and tragically painting God as a demanding despot who could neither be pleased nor pacified—a pernickety dictator. Their system was an exhausting waste of time, laughable if it had not been so tragic. These religious radicals put holiness beyond reach, and sin close at hand.

They had rules about how a guest at a wedding should greet the bride, and specific legislation about how to comfort a widow at a funeral. It was forbidden to glance into a mirror on the Sabbath, lest one catch sight of a stray gray hair, pull it out, and thus work on the day of rest.

The Pharisees postulated answers to questions that no one in his right mind would ever ask: Can I pray if I am working in the top of a tree? If I make some bread while I am naked, and I then want to use that bread for an offering, is it unclean? (A question that has troubled me for years.) Can a man divorce his wife for burning a meal? Is a person ceremonially unclean for touching a mouse? The Pharisees gave a tenth of the produce of their spice gardens, though it was never required by the Law, and they turned the simple act of eating into a nightmare.

Because they were radicals who wanted God's holiness to be expressed in every area of daily life, every meal became like an act of worship in the temple with a corresponding stack of regulations. The Pharisees had 229 texts about table fellowship, so many that some scholars describe them as "a table fellowship sect[4]." All food had to have been tithed on, and was carefully prepared with ritual hand washings. (It was on this point that the Pharisees clashed with Jesus and his disciples.[5]) The bizarre rules were not about hygiene; rather, they were strictly about ritual. Under Old Testament law, Aaronic priests were required to ceremonially wash their hands before stepping into the Tent of Meeting,[6] and the elders of a city were required to do the same if there was an unsolved murder case.[7] But religion always wants to take God's requirements and add to them. So the scribes and the Pharisees insisted on a complicated routine during everyday meals. Water, enough to fill ten eggshells, was first poured on both hands, which were held open with the fingers pointing upwards to run up the arm as far as the wrist, where it had to drop off because it was now unclean. Then the process had to be repeated with the fingers pointing down. Finally, each hand was cleansed by being rubbed with the fist of the other. A strict Pharisee would do this both before a meal and in between each course.

All of this rigmarole, absurd as it seems to us, was surely developed because of a genuine desire to honor God. But what was birthed by zeal had matured into a monster. Now the simple delight of a meal shared with family and friends was draped in dour legalistic demands. Also, a greater problem had developed: since the meal became an act of purification and worship, one could no longer share it with anyone who might "defile" the proceedings. Radical holiness turned into extreme exclusivity.

The Pharisees clashed with Jesus and guarded the meal table with a legalistic ferocity that was not just fuelled by pomposity (although they had plenty of that: we religious people are too often susceptible to arrogance), but genuine fervor and zeal. Much of their madness—and resulting blindness—actually stemmed from hearts set on pleasing God. Because of the constant sparring between Jesus and the Pharisees, we can rush to demonize them altogether—easy targets to hiss at. But the worrying truth is that, for the most part, their intentions were initially noble. For them, change would have signaled compromise and betrayal of God himself. Again, these were good people gone wrong.

How often do we who are passionate have *our* zeal hijacked? Earlier we met a passionate, zealous Pharisee called Saul who had participated in the stoning of Stephen.[8] His crime was heinous, but what is more chilling is this—Saul genuinely thought he was doing God a favor as he held the coats of those who threw rocks at the tormented Stephen. It was *zeal,* he later remarked to the Philippians, that fuelled his persecution of the church.[9] Religious zealots have consistently ruined the world in the name of God, and they still do.

Religious zeal birthed the nightmare of the medieval Crusades. The conquistadores felt that they were justified as they forced "conversion" to Christianity upon the native population of South America, where "converts" were baptized at sword point. And the modern missionary movement of the eighteenth and nineteenth centuries was prompted to acts of heroic sacrifice, but was also carried along with a nationalistic fervor that looks perilously close to Western imperialism.[10] It was an unwavering commitment to "godly principles" that enabled the British Victorians to hang children for stealing bread. Defenders of apartheid in South Africa often used the Bible to support their racist cause. Zealots can be highly dangerous, whatever the brand of their religion. Those who piloted a couple of airplanes into the World Trade Center on 9/11, irrevocably changing the world for the worst, are tragic examples of zeal gone wrong.

When good people, initially embracing the best intentions, turn bad, they turn faith into a formidable fortress. It is dark and gloomy inside, dimmed by impossible and meaningless rules and regulations.

A DISTURBING CHALLENGE

As we realize that the big brother was a good kid turned bad, and that the Pharisees—the very people that his character represents—were just like him, we are forced to face an inconvenient truth, one that is simple, obvious, but that may just be the last notion that occurs to us: *we* may be wrong.

Let's take it a step further: We *are* wrong. The Bible is God's inspired Word, but there is not one among us who is remotely close to being absolutely right in our understanding and interpretation of it. Some of our cherished, long-held convictions need to be taken out and aired, subjected to critique and evaluation, and discussed without arrogance or defensiveness.

Perhaps some of us have never taken time to examine some of those strong convictions that we have about the way our faith should be expressed. It might be that we have never taken the time or the effort to do so—legalism often thrives where there is laziness. It's easier and less intellectually demanding to toe the line than it is to ask the awkward questions. Perhaps we've inherited bad, hand-me-down ideas from good, genuinely godly people, and we feel that to question the validity of those notions is to betray them. But if that's the case, then a false loyalty has been created. It may be that in your church questions are discouraged, and those who suggest that the community's peculiar rules and regulations are beyond the scope of Scripture are viewed as compromisers or, worse still, enemies of the unity of the church. Sadly, some leaders create an atmosphere in churches where to ask a question is a sign of rebellion.

As we continue to look at the big brother, we'll see stubbornness, hypocrisy, unholy gossip, and a host of other sins — any or all of which we may share. But for now, perhaps we should face this simple and perhaps traumatic possibility: We may be wrong, no matter how long we've been in the faith or how mature in that faith we consider ourselves to be.

Chapter 8

CAPRICCIO: THE "ADVANCED" CHRISTIAN

Capriccio: A quick, improvisational, spirited piece of music.

Who is wise and understanding among you? Let him show it by his good life, by deeds done in the humility that comes from wisdom.

JAMES 3:13

He sat opposite me on the London train, looking rather dour. But it was his lapel badges that caught my attention. One was a little silver dove, and next to it sat a badge in the shape of a fish. Either this rather unhappy-looking man was a pigeon-fancying member of the National Fish Fryers Association, or he was a brother. I decided to venture the question.

I cleared my throat nervously. "Good morning ... er ... I noticed your lapel badges ..."

He stared back at me, unsmiling, silent. Yikes. Maybe he was more into cod than God. In for a penny, I thought, and so I continued.

"The badges ... those nice badges you're wearing. Do they mean that you are a Christian?"

He paused before responding, and looked me up and down with a disdainful glare that one might usually reserve for a person who makes bad smells in public. There was not a hint of warmth in his response, which was very much to the point.

"Yes."

Thus he succinctly affirmed his faith and said no more. I was a little taken aback. I didn't expect him to throw himself headlong across the carriage, scoop me up in a bear hug, and for us both to launch into a time of happy singing, but a little warmth wouldn't have been out of place either.

The silence was long. I desperately stammered into another question, asking him which church he attended. He named the church and then rather sniffily told me that he wasn't terribly happy with it, seeing as he was more *advanced* than everyone else in the congregation. "More advanced" sounded like an incongruous term to use for discipleship; it seemed more suited to a follower of karate than an apprentice of Christ. What constituted advanced Christianity? Did he know a little Greek? Had he mastered the art of walking on water, or was he a handy turn at parties, being able to change a bottle of sparkling water into a magnum of vintage champagne? I ventured further.

"Really. So ... how do you become an *advanced* Christian, then?"

"Well," he retorted, "I've been to a number of events and conferences that have helped me to become ... advanced. Like something called Spring Harvest, for example."

Now I was really interested. Spring Harvest is an annual Christian conference held in the United Kingdom, attracting some fifty thousand delegates. As a member of the leadership team responsible for the event, I told him that I "did a bit" with Spring Harvest.

"Really?" he said, and he leaned forward as if to whisper a secret. "Then let me tell you something," he said. "The next station after this is Pulborough Station. And that station is *Jeff Lucas's station*. He lives around these parts, you know. And that's his station." I decided to break cover, and so I told him my name. Jeff. Lucas. That's me.

"No you're not!" he exclaimed, and for a moment I thought that he might be right, seeing as he was more advanced than me. I assured him that I was who I thought I was. He warmed up a little, but not much. Moments later, he left the train. I hesitate to judge him. Perhaps he was having a bad day—or a tragic one. No one knows what a stern look may hide. But all that rather pompous stuff about being a Christian (an advanced, turbo-charged disciple) is difficult to defend.

As he left, a lady boarded the train, her husband and baby in tow. She didn't look like she had very much, and she couldn't speak English, her words suggesting she was from somewhere in Eastern Europe. As she cradled her baby in her arms, suddenly she launched into a soft lullaby, and within seconds I recognized the melody of Isaac Watts's beautiful hymn:

At the Cross, at the Cross
Where I first saw the light
And the burden of my heart rolled away
It was there by faith I received my sight
And now I am happy all the day.

I looked across at her, and she beamed back, a lovely, warm-hearted smile. As the train trundled on through the grey, dour smokestacks of South London, I think I realized what being "advanced" really means.

It's knowing that we've been kissed by grace and serenaded with gentle love. It's being grateful that we've been given what we could never earn, and offering a kindly smile that can change someone's day.

Chapter 9

GALLIARD: FROM PARTING TO PARTYING

Galliard: Music written for a lively dance for two performers, written in triple time.

When he came near the house, he heard music and dancing…
LUKE 15:25

It is the heart that is not yet sure of its God that is afraid to laugh in His presence.
GEORGE MACDONALD[1]

The sun was slowly sinking behind the distant hills as he made his way home. That now-benign orange ball had been merciless that afternoon, broiling him and his workers as they worked as fast as the furnace heat would allow. His job was more about supervision than manual labor—this family had servants to do the backbreaking work—but nonetheless, his body ached with that pleasant pain we feel after a job well done. At last he saw the warm, welcome lights of home in the distance, flickering against the gathering grey.

Then his ear caught something in the air: a deep, rumbling sound. What *was* that? He cupped his ear, walked a little more briskly, and now, as he drew closer, he realized, to his amazement, what was going on.

There would be no quiet meal and early evening for him. He could distinctly make out the sounds of a small band: a flute, a mandolin, and the heavy, throbbing bass of a drum dominating both. There was the sound of clapping and cheering too. It was the last thing he expected. Stepping up his pace to a brisk jog now, big brother realized that a full-on party was being held at his house. It had been going on for quite some time, apparently; *now* it was in full swing. The quiet pleasantries, the polite "how is it with you, very well, thank you" chatter was over. The noise suggested that most of the community had shown up, with children and servants spilling in and out of the house. Why the party? What could have happened to prompt such a big blowout? Then it dawned on big brother. Not only was this spontaneous bash happening without his knowledge or say-so. No, there was something else. They'd started the party without *him*.

Hurrying now, he could see that new guests were arriving, waiting patiently in line as servants performed the traditional foot washings that both refreshed and welcomed. Then he heard the shrill sound of women letting out the *kaffeka* — the victory cry. As he ran up to the courtyard, he felt a mixture of frustration and confusion. The sounds both wooed and yet irritated him. He'd get to the bottom of this. Slowing to a more dignified pace, he marched into the courtyard, his shoulders upright, his face resolute, chin set firm, a man on a mission.

THE PRODIGAL-FRIENDLY CHURCH AND COMMUNITY

Slaughter the fattened calf. Fire up the grill. Quickly get the word out around the village: we're serving gourmet food here tonight, and everyone's invited. It's party time, and the menu is sumptuous.

Veal — fattened calf — was not only a rare delicacy, but to cook up a whole calf meant that the celebration was a community-wide event, feeding around two hundred people. In Bible times, a calf was killed only for very special occasions. It was considered food fit for a king, as King Saul demonstrated when he broke a fast in order to tuck into a feast of veal.[2]

What do you serve when God, accompanied by a couple of angels, shows up on your doorstep? When the Lord appeared to Abraham in Genesis, fattened calf was the dish of choice. Calf was offered to mighty kings, to mighty angels, and to the mighty God.[3] In almost every biblical example where fattened calf was served, it was offered by a person of lesser rank to someone more senior than they. A subject cooks for King Saul. Abraham orders the best food for God.

I said *almost*, because in the story of the prodigal, the esteemed figure of the father ordered this gourmet meal for his grimy, would-be slave of a son. Once again Jesus's listeners would have drawn breath, bracing themselves to hear of a *kezazeh*. But that had already been cancelled and a huge banquet was held instead. This party was loaded with symbolism, for it was an event that served to reconcile the son into the wider community, not just his own immediate family.

Salvation is a community event, a fact that we surely need to remember, living as we do in a culture that worships the needs and demands of the individual. Burger King invites us to enjoy our cheeseburgers "our way," and we can be tempted to believe that church is something similar, little more than a spiritual gas station that primarily exists to meet our needs and desires. But God has always fulfilled his purposes through individuals-in-community. Michael Griffiths laments the cult of individualism in the church: "Pick up a hymn book ... note how very many 'I' and 'my' hymns there are, and how relatively few 'we' and 'our' hymns there are, which are really suitable for congregational singing. Most of our hymns would be more suitable as solos! It is as if most Christians expect to fly solo to heaven with only just a little bit of formation flying from time to time."[4]

We can easily slip into the trap of reading Scripture through the lens of individualism, rather than as members of God's family. Our need to read the New Testament in the English language creates confusion, where *you* (the second person singular) and *you* (the second person plural, as in "you all") is the same word.

When we read "you" in the New Testament, we might jump to the conclusion that Scripture is addressing us specifically as individuals rather than as part of the corporate body. Many of us read Paul's words to the Ephesians about putting on the armor of God[5] and his instructions about desiring and using the gifts of the Spirit,[6] and feel that Paul is talking to me, a person, rather than all of us, the church.

Only a church that is given to "formation flying" can hope to be prodigal friendly. God, who as Trinity is God-in-community and hence has never been alone, created Adam and Eve to be together. After the chaos and scattering of Babel, God sent Abram on his epic trip in order to see a new community birthed: Israel, a nation for all nations. As their story unfolded, through Abraham, Isaac, Jacob, the formation of twelve tribes, the harsh persecution of Egypt, and then the epic exodus and the gathering together at Mount Sinai, we see not just the rescue of a huge number of refugees, but the birth of a *community* created for the purposes of God on his earth. Although God deals with individuals, he calls us as individuals to connect with our destiny in and through community.

God's relationships with humanity throughout history have always been expressed corporately—he has sought to engage with *people,* not only *persons.* That is not to suggest that individualism is wrong: God deals with us as unique individuals, and salvation is a result of personal faith. But as individuals we only discover the potential of our being *imago dei* (in the image of God) as we take our place among the people of God. This is how we have been designed, and there our uniqueness finds its God-created context.

We are now part of the grace-family called the people of God, and what a beautiful family it is. Together we cry, laugh, share our burdens, worship, grieve, pray, eat, and serve. And this community is no austere, formal bunch. We're famous for our parties—or at least we should be. The returning prodigal came home to a hoedown bash of a party, not a somber prayer meeting.

GOD, COMMUNITY, AND PARTIES

In my first book on prodigals, *Will Your Prodigal Come Home?,*[7] I outlined the wonderful truth that God loves the imagery of the party. Permit me to quote what I said here:

The breathtaking truth is this—there is a party planner at the heart of the universe; this is how he welcomes *his* returning prodigals ... For some Christians, the image of a party is negative. Let's face it, parties can be occasions of excess, where too much alcohol dulls the minds of usually sensible people and mad choices are made in that fog. But, risky though it might seem to some, God loves the imagery of a good party and consistently uses it in the inspired words of Scripture to point to his own nature and the reality that he calls his people to be a partying people.

The festivals of the Old Testament era were huge parties that wonderfully disrupted the working life of Israel as the people of God were called together to toast their love for God and for each other. The book of Deuteronomy includes a command that seems almost unlikely, it is such an invitation to unbridled joy: "Exchange your tithe for silver, and take the silver with you and go to the place the LORD your God will choose. Use the silver to buy whatever you like: cattle, sheep, wine or other fermented drink, or anything you wish. Then you and your household shall eat there in the presence of the LORD your God and rejoice."[8]

Here the Party Planner commands his people to celebrate, but with the words "anything you wish" allows them space to decide the specific elements of the party. And God himself is not the wallflower, the stoic unsmiling spectator or party pooper who sits every dance out because he is above that kind of thing.

Zephaniah, described by one commentator as the prophet obsessed with doom, pictures God as the one who skips and pirouettes for joy over his people. The NIV almost loses the sheer exuberance of it all: "The LORD your God is with you, he is mighty to save. He will take great delight in you, he will quiet you with his love, he will rejoice over you with singing."[9] The

Hebrew word used here translated "rejoice" means "to leap." Just as the father in the prodigal story jumps up and rushes out to meet his son, so God is portrayed as One who is able to freely demonstrate emotion.

Jesus introduced the episode of the lost son with a statement often misunderstood: "In the same way, I tell you, there is rejoicing in the presence of the angels of God over one sinner who repents."[10] Often it is preached that it is the angels that are doing all the celebrating, whereas this is not what this verse actually says. Rather it is in *"the presence of the angels"* that this joy breaks out — surely a reference to the central person in the royal court of heaven, our God himself. And then, in the series of three stories about things that got lost — a sheep, a coin, and a much-loved son — each of them includes not only the recovery of those items, but a celebratory party that followed. The sheep is found, and "when he finds it, he joyfully puts it on his shoulders and goes home. Then he calls his friends and neighbors together and says, 'Rejoice with me; I have found my lost sheep.' "[11] And then the coin is recovered, "and when she finds it, she calls her friends and neighbors together and says, 'Rejoice with me; I have found my lost coin.' "[12]

One might almost think that to throw a party over the recovery of a coin is a little extravagant. But the One who took the rather unusual step of beginning his ministry at a party (and the staggering step of making his first miracle the mass production of rather fine wine) insists on using the party analogy. Asked what the kingdom of heaven was like, he replied that it was like a party. And the future to come? It's described as a great party. Little wonder that Tony Campolo has used the term "party deity" to describe our awesome God.[13]

If we are to represent this joyful God well, then we must learn how to create partying churches. Returning prodigals must be welcomed into a church that knows how to authentically celebrate their return and toast the gracious God who welcomes them home. But before we consider what it means to be a partying church, perhaps we'd do well to consider what it *doesn't* mean, lest we create a lackluster affair that is embarrassing and superficial—and from which people go home early or stay reluctantly.

WHAT THE PARTYING CHURCH IS *NOT*

The analogy of the church service as "grand gathering" sometimes is used unhelpfully. I've heard too many preachers impose a formal dress code on their congregations using the flimsy argument that one wouldn't visit a president or a member of royalty dressed informally. Is casual dress then appropriate for an audience with the King of Kings, they ask? Even the party analogy could be unhelpful here, because it's usual to dress up specially for a party. But theology by analogy is faulty thinking and fatally flawed. Those who would visit Buckingham Palace or the White House are subject to protocols that have been established by tradition. Her Majesty and Mr. President demand special etiquette and attire when we're in their presence. But our God calls for none of this, and to demand that the church service be a place where everyone dresses up in his or her "Sunday best" has little or nothing to do with what he wants. He is the God who is interested in the heart rather than the suit.

I remember meeting a young woman who had fled the church and become a prodigal because she was advised that wearing Doc Marten boots wasn't godly—as if boot selection creates any response in heaven. And I confess to feeling sad when I've seen young teenagers garbed in somber black suits on Sunday morning. If this was their dress of choice, then fine. But I fear that, in many cases, they've been squeezed into a religious mold and would be considered "unspiritual" and even "rebellious" if they refused to comply with the dress code. The prodigal-friendly church is not a church where people dress up to go and see God. The issue is freedom, not uniform. If I choose to wear a suit on Sunday, then so be it; next week I might choose jeans. It doesn't matter to God, and that's what *is* important.

The party analogy also fails us when we conclude that every service should be a gathering of those who are happy to the brink of mild ecstasy. When I first came to America, I was invited to participate in a pep rally for the local high school football team. I went along, with no idea about what was to come. For thirty minutes we yelled motivational slogans at the gangly youths, who looked rather lost in their helmets and shoulder pads. As we sang our "we can do it because we're the best" songs and then actually shared a war cry (which affirmed that, figuratively speaking, we were going to annihilate the other team—but nicely, as we were Christians) the team slowly came to the belief that, truly, they were mighty men of valor who could triumph in the NFL.

Sometimes church descends into something similar. The worship leader becomes a cheerleader, enquiring about our collective emotional state ("Is everybody happy? Say amen if you are!"). Many of our songs suggest that we are always soaring on the thermals of victory like eagles, rather than spluttering around like beleaguered pigeons, which is how we occasionally feel. I remember with pain some of the songs we used to sing when I first became a Christian, which emphatically stated that happiness, 24/7, was demanded of all true disciples:

> *We want everybody to be happy*
> *We want everybody to be glad*
> *We want everybody to be happy in the Lord*
> *And we don't want anybody sad ...*

It was hardly a red-carpet welcome for people battling with depression. Another little ditty, not noted for its theology of suffering, was agonizingly awful:

> *It isn't any trouble just to s-m-i-l-e*
> *No it isn't any trouble just to s-m-i-l-e*
> *If you pack up all your troubles*
> *Then they'll vanish like a bubble*
> *If you only take the trouble*
> *Just to s-m-i-l-e*

But sometimes smiling *is* a hugely troublesome and difficult thing to do. There's a time to weep as well as laugh; thankfully, grinning continuously for God is not a demand that he makes upon his people. We'll see in a moment that fun and laughter are very much part of the partying, prodigal-friendly church, but that's not to say that we are always thrilled at life. With that qualification, let's affirm that the prodigal-friendly church will be a place of natural, easy laughter. God is pleased about that. After all, he invented fun, laughter, and the ability to play in the first place.

PARTYING COMMUNITY: FUN AND LAUGHTER

I had just completed a series of four Bible studies at a Christian conference. Our studies together had been relaxed, easy times. I had explored the text and punctuated the presentation with stories and anecdotes — some of them peppered with humor — to drive home the point. Afterwards, a couple of nervous-looking people approached me and expressed appreciation for the teaching. And then, looking this way and that, to make sure that they weren't being overheard, they grinned broadly. "My, we had some fun, didn't we?" they whispered conspiratorially, as if we had indulged in some incredibly furtive behavior instead of simply laughing in church. They began to giggle at the memory of some of the stories, and it was lovely to see their bright, shining eyes. As they talked, it became clear that they came from churches where fun was viewed with suspicion. And then, as if to justify their enjoyment, they added, "But we did learn so much too." I'm glad that they laughed and learned both, but it was sad that they had been taught that fun should be an undercover activity.

Some Christians fear laughter, believing that it is trivial or unworthy of them. Giggling is for children, they think, not for the mature sorts who are into deeper things. They become the "frozen chosen," passionate, serious-minded folk with well-worn Bibles and furrowed brows, but with whom you wouldn't want to share lunch, never mind eternity. They turn into corseted, trussed, gloomy souls, *believing* in joy, but never really *tasting* it. We all become what we believe our God is like, and theirs is endlessly stern. Not surprising, they turn out just like him.

Some of this stems from a long-standing battle that the Christian church has had with laughter. In some monastic circles, laughter and play were punishable offenses: "If a brother willingly laughs and plays with children, he will be warned three times; if he does not stop, he will be corrected with the most severe punishment."[14]

Laughter was viewed negatively by those who saw that every aspect of life had to be functional and productive. Gregory of Nyssa, a fourth-century church leader, dubbed laughter as an enemy of humanity, because "laughter is neither a word nor action ordered towards any possible goal."[15] The list of frowners goes on. Fifth-century orator John Chrysostom probably didn't employ humor in his sermons, viewing a laugh as a moment of indifference.[16] Laughter was condemned because it was felt that the involuntary surrender that comes with that belly-laughing, shoulder-shaking, slap-your-sides-and-laugh-out-loud mirth was unseemly for the good Christian. "Raucous laughter and uncontrollable shaking of the body are not indicative of a well regulated soul, or of personal dignity, or self-mastery," said fourth-century Basil the Great, who probably wasn't great to be around. Others thought that laughter was a sign of spiritual slackening,[17] or viewed it as a pollutant.[18]

DOES GOD LAUGH? DID JESUS?

Surely laughter is a glorious gift from God, and one, like all of his other gifts, that we should thoroughly and freely enjoy and be thankful for. As we laugh, we embrace humility, refusing to take ourselves too seriously, and knowing that God's grace kisses us bumbling fools who get it wrong more than we get it right. As we laugh, we experience the emotional and physical nourishment that only pure mirth can bring. As we laugh, we trust, suspending our anxiety about the bills for just a while as we simply enjoy the moment. Laughter is the cement of community, a sacrament of joy that we share—and perhaps a hint of the great banquet to come. The winsome beauty of a smile can beckon others to come and take their seats at the top table of God's love.

God is fun. Chris Blake asks the questions many of us have wondered about:

> Does God ever laugh? Is God good-natured? We must face it: we are not likely to fall in love with a grouchy, over-particular, inflexible God. If we see God's personality as humorless and robotic, we can come to believe that loving him will make us strange. We fear, with some justification, that sooner or later we too may be raining spittle on homosexuals. We cannot trust a gloomy God.[19]

Consider the hilarious occasion when God invited Adam to participate in the "game" of naming the animals. And think about the gift of human sexuality. A "functional" God could have created a mechanism for procreation that involved little more than a warm handshake at a certain time of the month. Instead he invented the bizarre, ridiculous, and quite wonderful mating ritual—sex—that is so very odd and creative and fun that some laugh out loud during love-making. The quirkiness of the creation speaks of the humor and brilliance of the Creator. In that sense, sex is prophetic, revealing something wonderfully playful about the One who dreamed up the whole idea. What a delightful person is our God.

Theologians agonize over the question, did Jesus ever laugh? Forgive me, but the question seems absurd, not least because the Bible doesn't bother to tell us things that are obvious. As the agent of creation, Jesus invented laughter; our ability to see the funny side is uniquely human, and is an aspect of being made in God's image. A much sought-after guest at dinner parties and a firm favorite with children, Jesus must have had the relaxed composure about him that is expressed in laughter and fun. Humorlessness is an unattractive trait, and as the expression of total and complete, flawless humanity—the ultimate human—Jesus laughed. Where he went, joy followed:

> Wherever Jesus went there seemed to be a celebration; the tradition of festive meals, at which Jesus welcomed all and

sundry, is one of the most securely established features of almost all recent scholarly portraits. He was ... making these meals and their free-for-all welcome a central feature of his program.[20]

The prodigal-friendly church is called to be the primary sign of the kingdom — a living banquet, a working model of life lived under the love and lordship of Jesus, and a party with an open-door policy where all are invited to come in from the cold and join in the fun. One writer compares the church to the twelfth-century character of legend, Robin Hood. In that story, the honorable and good King Richard is absent from the country, and so the land is ruled by his despicable brother, King John. Harsh taxation and national oppression lead Robin, Maid Marion, and a band of "merry men" to go underground — or specifically, into the undergrowth of Sherwood Forest. Their acts of defiance and charity (robbing the rich to give to the poor) keep alive the hope of the good king's return. They are a mischievous, subversive lot, characterized by their playful ability to laugh in the face of suffering, because they know that the reign of evil is temporary. As we delight in story, laughter, and outrageous celebration and kindness, we become living signs of the reign of Christ that is here, but is yet to come in its fullness.

In a Robin Hood analogy, Graham Tomlin boldly declares that gloomy churches will never make an impact — on the contrary:

The images Jesus used to describe the kingdom were always full of delight. It is like a feast with lavish food and great hilarity, or a woman finding a priceless lost necklace and throwing a party to celebrate. The picture of a bunch of outlaws celebrating with huge joyful meals deep in the forest in defiance of the false powers is the same kind of story. This is no stern, solemn king, exercising a humorless, cold, rule. It is the rule of the gracious host, inviting us into his home, the place where he is in charge, and where there is lots of deep, rich laughter. Miserable, gloomy and dull churches have simply missed the point.[21]

LAUGHTER AND BEING OURSELVES

The church is a family, and the party that we are called to throw is more like a family barbecue than a glittering tuxedo event. Our church family should be like home to us, a place where we can truly be ourselves. Laughter is a sure sign of our being at home, both with God and each other. And people desperately want to be part of a family like that. Witness the upsurge of reality television, together with the popularity of television series such as *Friends*. The opening theme song from the television series *Cheers*, popular in the 1980s, says it all about the desperate hunger for authentic relationships:

You wanna be where you can see, troubles are all the same
You wanna be where everybody knows your name

Churches that will create space for meaningful relationship, fun, and laughter will grow—and that includes returning prodigals who want to be part of them.

Recently a British student studied large, growing churches from charismatic and non-charismatic denominations, evangelical and historical/traditional backgrounds, and both the Protestant and Catholic elements of the Christian family. The research student was looking for the "X" factor in them all that might point to the main reason for their rapid growth. The study took a year, and finally he reached his conclusion. The common factor that each and every one of these fast-growing churches shared was that each was a community where people laughed together. Steve Chalke commented on the research project: "Each church provided the kind of environment in which people were relaxed enough to be able to laugh. You only really laugh when you can be yourself—when you feel comfortable."[22]

We must abandon the idea that prayer and Bible studies are *spiritual* and that social events—golf tournaments, movie evenings, barbecues—are less so. A pastor friend of mine announced to his church, "We're having a golf tournament this week. Now I know that's not terribly spiritual, but we'd like you to come anyway ..."

Stop right there. Who says that being together, sharing a sport, laughing and listening and relaxing and playing—that these aren't spiritual? We are people who can glorify God in everything we do. The only thing that is secular is sin.

HAVING FUN, SERIOUSLY

Laughter needs no defense. The health studies that have shown the multiple psychological and physiological benefits of laugher only serve to confirm what Christians and Jews already know from their Scriptures—laughter is good medicine. And there are even more benefits for a partying church that knows how to laugh. Humor is a tremendous vehicle for communication and learning: when we laugh, it's because we've understood the punch line or seen the funny side to the story. In short, we "get it." The relaxed atmosphere created by humor means that defenses come down, enabling us to be open to the activity of the Holy Spirit in our lives. Surely this is why the court jester in medieval times was such a vital and important figure. That fool was no fool: he was a brilliant, irreverent, and amusing critic to the king, an immensely powerful rogue who alone could nudge the mightiest power in the land to do the right thing all through his wit and repartee. He could speak bluntly, could tell the king exactly what the common people were thinking, and was confidant to some of the king's personal life that nobody else shared. Some jesters were even used as ambassadors and diplomats, navigating their way through intricate and tricky negotiations with their powerful humor and charm. The best jesters were handsomely rewarded and, in some cases, showered with honors, titles, pensions, and land. The jester taught with laughter and sought to bring healing to painful situations.

With an ability to laugh at ourselves, our churches would be able to steer their way through delicate and hurtful conflicts, and enable people to grow in their understanding of truth. All this could happen if the role of the jester/preacher/leader were more acknowledged and we abandoned our suspicion of the smile.

Tony Campolo reminds us that laughter is, in one sense, no laughing matter:

> There really isn't anything frivolous about having fun. Learning how to have fun is one of the most serious subjects in the world. Without fun, marriages don't work. When jobs aren't fun, they become intolerable and dehumanizing. When children aren't fun, they are heartbreaking. When church is not fun, religion becomes a drag. When life is not fun, it is hard to be spiritual.[23]

PARTY CHURCH—COLOR AND CREATIVITY

Earlier we saw that many prodigals leave for the far country simply because they are bored. The partying church will seek to express its message through the arts, which, sadly, are still held at arm's length by many Christians, who believe them to be "worldly" and inferior to preaching. But we serve the God who describes himself as the Creator; he is the one who not only originally created, but used colorful and creative "props" to jog the minds of his forgetful people. When church becomes monotone and dull, before long we forget why it is that we are part of it. We need colorful reminders of the reason for it all.

Michael Griffiths exposes the forgetfulness that we all battle in his pithy and prophetic book *Cinderella with Amnesia*:

> Christians collectively seem to be suffering from a strange amnesia. A high proportion of people who "go to church" have forgotten what it is all for. Week by week they attend services in a special building and go through their particular, time honoured routine, but give little thought to the purpose of what they are doing.[24]

This amnesia is a deadly disease that has threatened God's people throughout history. Israel, the Old Testament people of God, constantly lost sight of the plot, forgot who they were, and mislaid their God-given mission.

And so the Lord, "the great dramatist," used many props to nudge Israel to remember his bigger story. The story was to be gossiped in everyday life, not just expressed in formalized religious ceremonies. Rather, Israel was called to rehearse the script continually, at home, on the road, when resting or active. She tasted the story as she ate unleavened bread to celebrate the Passover. She scribbled the story on the doorposts of her houses. She wore the story, tying symbols on hands and foreheads, and she sang and danced the story too. The story was immortalized by commemoration, as altars and stone pillars were built to mark the spot of historic triumphs. Words were accompanied by rich and vivid symbols; Israelites had blood splashed over them as Moses read them the Law. The story was constructed by builders and curtain-makers in the development of the tabernacle and temple. Furniture makers carved the story in wood, sculptors sculpted it, metalworkers hammered it out, and jewelers set the story in precious stones. The story was smelled as incense was offered; it was acted out through the elaborate sacrificial system. It was chimed as the priestly bells sounded. Priests, with their colorful vestments, were lead players in the drama; the breastplate, turban, sash, and ephod called for embroiderers to stitch the story.

But the drama went further, cutting into Israel's time and flesh in the creation of the festivals and feasts, and the rite of circumcision. Circumcision was the sign of the covenant, the reminder of a union with God that made its mark to the very depths of the human psyche, faith impacting even that which is most private and hidden. Circumcision was a sign to the bearer that they were different. *You belong to God, and you exist for God's purposes. Don't forget it.*

Israel was also called to prioritize the covenantal celebrations, the sacred assemblies of Passover, Tabernacles, Firstfruits, Weeks,

Trumpets—and Sabbath, enabling the people to quite literally re-enact their history creatively. They would not just hear the story rehearsed in words, but would participate in a huge play where they were the actors and audience both. The Passover feast was to be eaten by a people dressed and ready for a journey, with cloaks tucked into their belts, sandals on their feet, and a staff in hand. A mass campout lasting seven days was required when the Feast of the Tabernacles was celebrated. It was not enough to hear the story of the nomadic journeying of their ancestors through the wilderness; the people had to live in booths made of tree boughs and the branches of palm trees for seven days so that they could experience something of what their predecessors experienced. How do we most effectively remember the passion of Jesus? Not through words, but by eating bread and drinking wine. It's not enough to talk about the death and resurrection that we experience through Christ; we *participate* in the minidrama of baptism as a visual aid. We *act out* the truth.

We, the people of God, are only able to fulfill our prophetic calling as long as we imbibe, rehearse, and live out God's story; without that story, we are like "salt that has lost its saltiness." When the dreaded amnesia sets in, the people of God become functionally useless or, as Jesus put it more plainly, "no longer good for anything." Then the world, denied the antiseptic, cleansing power of us salt-people, descends into greater rot and decay. And so God calls us to be a creative people, just like him.

But big brothers often don't agree.

HEALTH WARNING: BIG BROTHERS HATE PARTIES

Be warned: churches that look to prioritize fun, laughter, and relationships will certainly offend some people. I discovered that when preaching in one American church.

I was just about to leave the church after the service ended, when I realized that I had left my Bible open on the pulpit, my used sermon notes scattered at its side. I was tired, weary from the emotional and physical demands of travel and preaching, but was warmed by that pleasantly contented feeling inside that Christian leaders enjoy when it seems that the service has gone well. The atmosphere had been light and relaxed. I love to use humor when I preach, and the congregation had apparently enjoyed my use of fun and story. They responded in droves during the time of prayer at the end of the message. Some had become Christians. I felt good and grateful: ministry was fulfilling, worthwhile. The happy feeling would not last long. On my Bible sat a note, folded stiff with razor sharp creases, upright, demanding my immediate attention. Something told me that this was not fan mail. My stomach felt hollow as I opened the note. A shudder went through me as I quickly scanned it. It was written in a large, angry scrawl and—worst of all—it was unsigned.

Anonymous letters are like poison darts to preachers. They are usually written by people who do not have the courage to put their name to their opinions, and they are a devastating way to efficiently deliver a dose of vitriol. Sending an anonymous letter is like running up to someone in the darkness, punching them full in the face, then scooting off before they can even see who their attacker is.

The epic evangelist D. L. Moody once received an unsigned abusive note while he was preaching. An usher walked up to the pulpit and wordlessly handed the great man a scrap of paper with but one word written on it: *Fool.* Cool and clever, Moody placed the note on the lectern. "I've just received the most unusual communication. I often get letters from people who write the letter, but leave their signature off. This one is different. This sender forgot to write the letter, but just signed his name."

My letter contained more than one word.

> *Sir, we would see Jesus not your comedy act and nonsensical gibberish. You can't win souls to Jesus with all that nonsense. You are not a preacher, you are a comedian. You have missed your calling.*

I folded the note and fought back tears: no one enjoys being so marginalized. Bumping into big brother types, some of whom have been systematically taught over many years to regard fun and laughter with suspicion, isn't easy. But I do know this: I'm happy to be a fool, whatever the big brothers think. The prodigals need a party. And when they find one, they can laugh their way back into life ...

... Sometimes literally.

Chapter 10

VIVACE: LAUGHING
OUR WAY BACK TO LIFE

Vivace: Direction to performer to play a composition in a brisk, lively, and spirited manner.

Gemma knew that the poor woman only had a few minutes of life left. Doris, a thin, elderly lady, had been rushed into the emergency room in the middle of the night. The ER doctor on duty had called the ward where Gemma was charge nurse with an urgent and kindly request. Knowing that the end was near, he wanted to spare Doris the indignity of dying on a hospital cart in a curtained-off cubicle, under the cold glare of fluorescent strip lights. He wanted her to breathe her last in the warm comfort of a bed, with the lights dimmed a little, and her family gathered around her. But death was stalking Doris and moving in fast. She was deeply comatose and losing a fight to breathe normally—her vitals were simply closing down. The doctor said she had twenty minutes at most, and that she probably wouldn't survive the elevator ride up to the ward. Make her comfortable, he said.

The hospital orderly arrived and wheeled Doris into a side room, quickly followed by her distraught family members. Gemma and the orderly carefully lifted Doris into the bed. Gemma puffed the pillow beneath her head, adjusted her oxygen mask, and spoke gently to Doris's family. *Hold her hand, now. Whisper quietly to her if you like. It won't be long.* Gemma stepped out of the room to allow them to share the intimacy of death in private.

That's when everything went so terribly wrong, or so it seemed. Gemma sat quietly outside the room, and just then another nurse arrived and began a conversation with her. She told how she had gotten hopelessly lost driving to a job interview that day. Looking for a hospital, she had ended up in a local park and managed to drive her car right onto a carefully manicured lawn. The more the story unfolded, the more Gemma laughed. What began as a stifled behind-the-hand giggle turned into a deep, raucous belly laugh. Gemma begged her friend to stop her story, but to no avail. Not one normally given to laughing out loud, Gemma howled and roared for quite some minutes, the sound of it echoing down the dark linoleum corridor. But as she laughed uncontrollably, she realized that, behind the thin drywall, just a few feet away, a lady was dying, relatives were weeping, and her laughter was not only out of place—it would probably get her fired. She dried her eyes and steeled herself to apologize to the family for her wholly inappropriate behavior.

But as she opened the door, Gemma was met with an unbelievable sight. Doris was sitting up in bed, laughing. She had removed her oxygen mask, and was now giggling at her stunned relatives. "Are you ... are you alright?" asked Gemma, amazed.

"Well dear," said Doris, her eyes sparkling. "I heard this sound of beautiful laughter, and I wanted to join in. The laughter was so lovely, so infectious, so I laughed along, woke up, and here I am. Are you the one with the lovely laugh?" The delightful conversation that followed revealed that both Gemma and Doris are Christians.

Gemma didn't lose her job, and Doris didn't lose her life. The next day the doctors pronounced her perfectly fit enough to go home. She is well as I write this. She laughed her way back into life.

We can do the same. Don't stifle that smile or apologize for having fun, for we too can laugh our way into life.

If in doubt, ask Doris.

Chapter 11

STACCATO: AN ANGRY YOUNG MAN COMES HOME

Staccato: Short, detached notes, as opposed to legato, which means to play smoothly.

So he called one of the servants and asked him what was going on.

"Your brother has come," he replied, "and your father has killed the fattened calf because he has him back safe and sound."

The older brother became angry and refused to go in.
LUKE 15:26–28

He probably put the question to one of the children in the courtyard, for the word "servant" isn't the best translation. One version describes the encounter like this: "So he asked one of the lads ..."[1] At parties like this, children too young to enter the banquet enjoyed playing outside. Whoever the big brother spoke with, his question shows that he was bewildered and confused. That his father would throw a welcome-home party for his wayward kid brother was completely beyond his comprehension. It was inappropriate, such a wanton waste of hard-earned cash.

Sadly, the elder brother had forgotten what "stuff" is for. The calf had been fattened for one reason alone—to feed partying guests and (in the father's thinking) to nourish half-starved homecoming prodigals. But big brother had lost the plot. He summoned the young lad, his blazing eyes probably causing the child to quickly scamper across the courtyard, perhaps fearful of a rebuke.

Our translation of the boy's report, "He has him back safe and sound," doesn't do justice to his meaning. The party wasn't thrown because the prodigal had returned from the far country without serious injury; indeed, in the far country, the wayward lad had admitted that he was *dying* of hunger, so this was not a party to celebrate good physical health. The boy's report to the older brother includes the concept of *shalom*: someone received back with peace. He has been truly received home. He is fully back in the fold. At this news, big brother ignited. A party started without him was irritating, but a party for that ex-brother of his was an outrage.

To Near Eastern listeners, what happens next is yet another shocking development. The elder brother should have immediately entered the banqueting hall, where he too would have been welcomed with cheers, handshakes, and compliments from the guests. He could then withdraw briefly to bathe, change his clothes, and then rejoin the party, where, as we will see, he would exercise a special role in the evening's proceedings.

But he explodes with anger and refuses to go in.

As big brother flies off the handle — the word *angry* means to be enraged — the music stops suddenly. The joyful songs fade in the throats of the singers and, perhaps, inside the house, the prodigal, so relieved and thrilled by the welcome, feels fear in the pit of his stomach. He knew that all of this was just too good to be true. He recognizes the sound of that screaming voice. Big brother has woken him out of his dream, and now he faces the rejection he'd been expecting all along. This was a crisis. Who knows? If the man outside has his way, this could turn into *kezazeh*.

A REACTIONARY HOTHEAD

Rather than taking time to respectfully ask his father some questions about the party, big brother explodes with rage after a chat with a child. Big brothers sometimes do that not because they are thoughtful or reasonable, but because of a tendency to react rather than respond. When we insist on taking a simplistic view of things and rush to rage rather than taking time for thoughtful, prayerful process, conflict results. When a prodigal returns with a messy life, leaving a wake of pain, addiction, and need, big brother often doesn't see the person. He just smells the stink and concludes that the church is for good people, that bad people will mess that up, and the church should stay clear of them unless they get themselves sorted out fairly quickly.

Later in the story, we see that big brother completely misunderstood the reason for the party, believing it to be in honor of his brother. It was not. The banquet was no attempt to paper over the cracks of the prodigal's behavior and turn him into a returning hero; rather the party was in honor of the father. It was his magnanimous, spectacular grace that sat at the heart of the joyous event. The woman's party is not in honor of a coin any more than the shepherd throws a bash to honor a sheep. In all three cases, the call was to celebrate a finding, not to honor the thing, animal, or person found.

The prodigal-friendly church is a messy celebration of the Father's love, not a cheap denial of the severity of sin. But the elder brother didn't see that—he was too busy reacting, huffing and puffing, and most likely wanting to blow the house down.

Earlier we talked about the need for relevant, provocative preaching. Because of the reactionary nature of the elder-brother types, some churches are never able to broach difficult subjects, because certain key words become triggers that ignite an explosion. Here are some of the trigger topics most likely to create an instant fuss in the American church (churches in other nations, such as Britain, have their own sensitive issues, of course).

- *Environment* (This climate change hocus-pocus is a myth dreamed up by liberals—and, hey, the planet's gonna burn anyway.)
- *Tithing* (Oh no, they're after my money again.)
- *Homosexuality* (Why mention it, preacher? What's to say except "stop that"?)
- *Drinking alcohol* (Good Christians don't do that. Yes, Jesus turned water into wine, but that wasn't his best day.)

Not only is the elder brother reactionary, but he often ends up talking to the wrong person. When we insist on widely airing our complaints and concerns around the church, and "sharing" our nervousness about returning prodigals with all and sundry rather than talking out our very real worries with leaders who can make a substantial response, we risk tearing apart what God is trying to build. The picture of the elder brother in conference with the boy reminds us to avoid gossip, especially the kind when we talk to a wide number of people, insisting with each of them that they keep our conversations private under the shield of confidentiality, while we gradually, quietly poison others. Let's think rather than explode; let's talk out our nervousness, if we have any, with the right people.

POWER, CONTROL, AND SERVANTHOOD

In his courtyard chat with the child, big brother was turning into a bosslike figure, demanding an explanation for his father's action, when in reality his father owed him no explanation at all. It was *his* money, he could do with it what he liked. Ironically, just as the prodigal son had begun his downward trek by telling his father how to spend money ("Give me!"), now big brother does essentially the same thing, upset as he is about the cost of the extravagant party. One ancient commentator spots the control-freak behavior of the elder brother, who "asked for the reasons for the banquet as though the family had no right to set up such a banquet in his absence, whereas he should have entered the hall and shared the joy of those who were rejoicing."[2]

In reality, the eldest brother's responsibility went beyond merely attending the banquet—he was supposed to serve at it. In the culture of the day, the eldest brother of the house was required to take a role not dissimilar to that of a head waiter. He would circulate while the food was being served, talking to and welcoming the guests, and honoring them with his service and personal attention. But big brothers often "graduate" from being servants to becoming controllers instead.

Sometimes I'm able to spot the controlling "barons" in a church where I'm the guest speaker. If I say something that is a little controversial, I often notice that many in the congregation turn and look over at one person in the crowd to see how they react. If the baron nods in agreement or laughs at the joke, then they nod too, or risk a guffaw. But if the baron looks stony-faced, then the others, somewhat sheeplike, follow suit. Of course the one being watched may simply be considered highly respected and trustworthy. But it can also indicate that someone is taking inappropriate control and is setting himself up as an unauthorized power base.

The church belongs to God. There is but one Lord of this particular manor, and he can do what he likes. He alone is the One with the absolute right to take charge. We must refuse the temptation to choreograph or manage him, which is the recurring blunder that we humans are so prone to make. At the beginning of his epic trek with God, Moses had to know first and foremost that the Lord was the "I am,"[3] the One who is who he is and will be who he will be.

That's always the starting point in any journey with God. Too often we are like those tiny people in *Gulliver's Travels*. We scurry around, frantically trying to pin down the giant, eager to peg his strong arms to the ground with our pygmy thinking, our religious protocols, and our miniaturized expectations. And if that idea is too much of a stretch for us, let's at least admit that we'd like to be God's manager and steer him "rightly." Like the bumbling disciples who tried to shoo clamoring, giggly children away from Jesus,[4] we risk his anger with our fussing. More than just irritated, Jesus was "indignant" with his inept team. Some translators use the word "incensed" to describe Jesus's reaction; nothing much meek and mild there.

Peter the control freak tried to steer Jesus away from the cross,[5] the very place Jesus had to go so that everyone everywhere could be welcomed at God's table. Jesus tagged Peter as acting like Satan, because he tried to maneuver Jesus away from the very work that would throw open the gates of the kingdom. It was a warning for us all not to stand in the way of God's program to invite every-one to know his love. In another instance in the Bible, furious Jonah[6] traded in his ticket to Nineveh for a one-way trip to Tarsh-ish—and a spell in a rather fishy submarine. Why? Because he thought he knew better than God. The disciples[7] made a stink and reached for a calculator when that precious, oh-so-pricey perfume was poured over Jesus's feet. All of these and many more were guilty of the same basic sin of trying to control the Lord. As the saying goes, God made us in his own image, and ever since we've been trying to return the favor.

We can rush to take inappropriate ownership of our churches, thinking them to be "ours" in the wrong sense. We must come to the place where we abandon our cherished hopes that God will fit into our boxes, our expectations, our ways. He is outrageous, he will welcome whom he will welcome, and although he needs no permission from us to do what he does, in order to make the party really swing he awaits our permission. We are fellow guests at the table. Without our partnership the party will be a dour affair. Or perhaps it might even be cancelled.

Power broking comes in subtle guises. I've seen big brothers disguise themselves as "weaker brothers," leaping on Paul's words about not causing a weaker brother to stumble or be offended.[8] They then complain that *they* are offended by the music, the change of service schedule, and indeed any change that the church might make that is not to their personal preference. A *weaker* brother is usually a younger Christian with a weak conscience; the elder brother is often a veteran of faith with overly strong personal pref-erences. We'd do well to know the difference.

DOES BIG BROTHER KNOW BEST?

When we act like elder brothers, we can be bullish and stub-born. Ironically, the more that some try to persuade big brother to come around and think a little more about his reactions, the deeper he might dig his heels in, feeling that he is one of the staunchly faithful few left. In the prodigal story, big brother broadcasts his anger widely by his refusal to enter the banquet—a very public refusal.

Years ago I bumped into a big-brother type who didn't appreciate my pastoral leadership. Whenever I preached, which was on most Sundays, he would stand up, pick up his chair, and face it towards the side wall. When the sermon was completed, he would turn the chair back again to face the front. And then, on the way out of the church building, as I stood in the foyer shaking hands, he would always leave me with a bitter comment that felt like a punch in the face.

One Sunday, as he shook my hand while leaving, he delivered one of his usual verbal slaps. But instead of letting go of his hand, I held on to it. I could feel the tears coming, and the months of pain welling up. The floodgates opened and I stood there, holding his hand, sobbing uncontrollably. Suddenly he saw the fruit of what he had been doing and apologized continuously, so anxious was he to make amends. He never turned his chair to the wall again. But it took a hugely embarrassing moment—for him as well as me—to shake him out of his stubborn behavior. We must face the unpalatable truth that religious people can at times be even more hard-hearted than those who profess no faith in God.

A willingness to listen and an openness to being persuaded: these are the qualities that should characterize God's people. Sometimes we disguise our obstinacy by declaring that we are simply refusing to compromise, when in fact we are just being stubborn and are unwilling to change our minds. We can be wooden and inflexible.

Chick Yuill describes the lovely attitude of Eric Liddell, the famous athlete whose story inspired the movie *Chariots of Fire*:

> He ... was willing to give up the chance of a gold medal in the one hundred meters at the 1924 Paris Olympics because of his strict adherence to the principle of Sunday observance. But few of us are aware that Liddell, having gone to China as a missionary, died a relatively

young man just over twenty years later in a Japanese prisoner of war camp, towards the end of World War 2. There was some freedom of activity allowed within the confines of the camp, and, because of his achievements and reputation, Liddell was given responsibility for overseeing and organizing sporting activities. His biographer relates an incident which is seemingly trivial, but is actually very significant.

One of the hardest decisions he had to make in the camp was what to do about Sunday games. No, he said, there would be no games on Sunday; it was a principle from which he had never deviated. But many of the teenagers protested about this and decided to organize a hockey game by themselves without him—boys against girls. It ended in a free fight, because there was no referee. It is a most illuminating detail of his life: he would not run on a Sunday for an Olympic gold medal in the 100 meters and all the glory in the world; but he refereed a game on a Sunday, he broke his unbreakable principle, just to keep a handful of imprisoned youngsters at peace with each other. It speaks volumes about the man.[9]

The elder brother showed no such openness and flexibility.

He had it in his power to destroy the banquet, to smear his father's good name, and turn the happy festivity into an embarrassing fiasco. When a big brother is out of control, terrible things can happen.

Including attempted murder.

Chapter 12

AGITATO: KILLER KING—WHEN ANGER GETS THE BEST OF US

Agitato: A directive to perform the indicated passage in an agitated, hurried, or restless manner.

Fifteen hundred years before Jesus told the prodigal story, a big-brother type sat on the throne of Israel. Saul was tall, dark, and handsome, and he had a love/hate relationship with one of his musicians. On good days, Saul enjoyed David's harp playing, finding it soothing to the soul. But his bad days were very bad indeed, because the king had developed the habit of lobbing spears at David, a retired shepherd boy who occasionally killed Philistine giants. Elder brothers can form dangerous pressure groups, but when there's a big brother parked in the palace, watch out.

It was David's victory over verbose Goliath and the resulting adulation that had sparked such a murderous reaction from jumpy, insecure Saul. It all began with the daily humiliation of jeers and taunts from the gigantic champion. Saul knew that he was no match for this muscular prizefighter with a mouth to match. For six awful weeks, Saul and his army had shouted war cries, run up and down hills, and drawn up battle lines—but still there was no one among them to take on Goliath.

Then an upstart shepherd boy appeared on the scene, seemingly out of nowhere, with a mad idea: in God's strength, he'd tackle mighty mouth. At first Saul protested. How could a spindly sheep hand stand a chance against such a seasoned prizefighter as Goliath? When David declared that he really believed he could take the guy, Saul did what big brothers often do: he insisted that David wear Saul's armor. And so, probably with some of the pomp and ceremony much beloved of kings, the armor was strapped onto the lad. But there were two problems. First, the armor that Saul had such confidence in simply *hadn't worked* for Saul. He was resolutely committed to that which had been patently ineffective. Big brothers in our churches often do that, clinging to programs that don't work, methods that don't deliver, events that don't reach anyone, and notions that haven't helped them live their Christian lives one jot. Then they demand that everybody else do what has never worked for *them*. Second, the armor didn't fit David, so he was clunking around, restricted by an ungainly getup that was never made for him in the first place.

The next part of the story is well known. Goliath showed up and shouted his usual drivel, while David reached for his trusty sling, the one that he'd used so many times before (as a bear and lion discovered to their peril). The lad picked up five stones, but only needed one, prompting many to speculate: Why five? Did the number have a special meaning? Did Goliath have four ugly brothers? Perhaps the answer is more obvious, more human. Perhaps David took four extra stones just in case he missed with the first one. Of course he didn't miss. Goliath tumbled, and David took home the giant's head as a grisly souvenir. The nation was ecstatic, Saul included.

But the king's exhilaration died quickly. Perhaps he felt displaced, out of control, and dishonored. And then the people had started to sing *that* song.

"Saul has slain his thousands, and David his tens of thousands."

At times, his anger was too much to bear, and Saul tried his hardest to pin David to a wall with a spear. Saul tried to eliminate the very person that God had placed his hand upon; David would be a mighty leader and king. Just as big brothers ultimately lent a helping hand to those who killed Jesus, so Saul almost succeeded in wiping out a man who would lead Israel through the golden years.

Grace is infuriating. It's not fair. It invites people that we don't like to know love, success, and blessing. Let's be careful of that big brotherly anger. It can kill.

Chapter 13

PIZZICATO: THE NEW FAMILY PRODIGAL

Pizzicato: Plucking instead of bowing a string instrument.

> *So his father went out and pleaded with him. But he answered his father, "Look! All these years I've been slaving for you and never disobeyed your orders. Yet you never gave me even a young goat so I could celebrate with my friends."*
>
> LUKE 15:28–29

It all happened in less than a second, as the sentence rolled off the master storyteller's tongue. As in all the best dramas, suddenly, in a shocking moment, everything changed. Roles switched in a stunning hairpin turn. The prodigal, recently so very far away, was restored, safe in the house, reconciled to his father, thrilled by the party, if not somewhat concerned about the fracas taking place outside.

Big brother had suddenly taken his place and become the new prodigal. For the second time that day, the father had to go out to a wayward son, but this one showed no signs of wanting to join the party. Big brother was outside the house and intent on staying there. One Near Eastern scholar offers this translation: "His father came out searching for him." That word *searching* is the same word used to describe the action of the shepherd and the woman earlier in the story.

Suddenly the gang of muttering Pharisees, listening intently to every word that Jesus spoke, were confronted with a mirror image of themselves. Those listening realized by now that "he"—the older son — represented *them*. But the prodigal son, of course, represents all of us; indeed, this is a story of *two* prodigal sons.

Sadly, only one of them realized it.

PRODIGALS ALL

There is a well-known Arabic phrase regarding this story that says "each one of them is worse than the other." How apt that Near Eastern logic applies to these two brothers.

We've touched on this before, but it's a critical point: If we are to create truly prodigal-friendly churches, we must realize that we're all in the same boat, all grubby people in the process. The parable uses the imagery of distance poignantly: both sons start from the place of being outside; both try to act like servants. The younger wanted to work off his debt, and the elder, while all along a son, has lived like a slave for years, at least in his head and heart. Both demand payment in the story — either his share of the inheritance or a goat for a private party. Each one wanted something from the father to satisfy his own interests. Each insults his father, although, as we'll see, big brother's insult is greater, a public shaming. Both attempt manipulation, and each one moves towards a community away from the father and the father's friends — the prodigal to the far country, and the elder brother towards his pals with whom he wants to share a barbecue. To each, the father shows his costly, sacrificial, patient love, even as each of them has threatened the unity of the entire family by their selfishness. Both are prodigals.

When we think about creating prodigal-friendly churches, we do so as those who share the same common need for grace. That grace is not just needed for other people, out in the distance somewhere. We do not patronizingly decide to show kindness to them, but seek to show the same mercy that we have been shown and continue to experience day by day. The saved are yet sinners, who continue on the journey of recovery. There's a robe of salvation on our shoulders, but only grace placed it there, and it will be grace, as the old hymn says, that will ultimately carry us home. We'll look closer at the pleading father later, as he gently, sweetly tries to coax his son into the house. For now, let's focus on this strange sight of a new prodigal—a prodigal in the pew.

PRODIGAL BIG BROTHER: LIVING LIKE A SLAVE

The temptations all Christians wrestle with extend beyond sin's enticing and hollow promises. For the prudent, the faithful, and the zealous, the more subtle temptation of religious slavery awaits, a well-camouflaged trap that has snapped over the heels of too many. Driven by our false notions of what God is like, not only do some of us work ourselves into the ground, but we labor joylessly, sullenly convinced that God can never quite be appeased. For some, God by default is angry, and somehow needs to be persuaded to love. That God is a heartless despot. He is the God of the wall plaque that I recently spotted, which read, "If you want to hear God laugh, tell him your plans." Surely this is a twisted notion, as if our hopes, aspirations, and dreams are of no worth to our heavenly Father, and that he somehow delights in deriding and mocking them. Those with such a view of God often spend years—tragically, in some cases, a lifetime—frantically doing things for him. The deeper tragedy is that God never asked them to do those things in the first place. He isn't looking for slaves, only adopted sons and daughters.

When the prodigal returned home and presented his entirely logical plan to join his father's workforce, Dad would have none of it. It wasn't even a matter for discussion, and the offer was turned down flat, without any further explanation. It was simply unacceptable to the father to have one of his sons as a slave. But big brother, having worked for years with the heart and mind of a slave, blames his father for his condition. He goes on to blatantly malign his father too, complaining that he's never been given even a young goat; whereas, in fact, he'd been handed the title deeds to two-thirds of the entire farm. The elder brother had lived beneath his privileges for too long. As resentment seeped into the big brother's heart, not only is he incensed with his younger sibling, he is irate with his father too—just as the Pharisees were angry and critical of Jesus.

Likewise, when we live similarly as Christians, the whole experience becomes a tedious trek. We can grow angry at God and resentful of anyone living a more exciting and fulfilled Christian experience than we are—like that returning prodigal experiencing extravagant grace, for example. We may realize that we've lost a lot of our lives fretting about things that God never asked us to concern ourselves with. Perhaps we unthinkingly downloaded demands from zealous humans, demands that are far from the heart of God. It's one thing to have spent too many years in slavery, but don't continue your jail term by hurling unwarranted slander at God.

Near Eastern commentators have noticed that the big brother never uses the common greeting "O father," as respect and intimacy would demand in that culture. He just launches into an abusive tirade. Big brothers are often faithful in church, conscientious givers, morally scrupulous, and doctrinally orthodox. But they have lost the astonishment that should be the permanent condition of the forgiven sinner. The spiritual honeymoon is long over, and now they live in a worn-out marriage to God, where there is no intimacy, spontaneity, and very little conversation. The marriage continues, but more because of fear and duty. The wonderful father figure in the story first offers himself to his young son; now, as he goes out to plead with his eldest boy (rather than hastily dispatching a servant with an order to sort out the troublemaker), we see that the father offers himself to his older son too. If our hearts have become cold, indifferent, and unmoved—and so we have become prodigals in the pew—then God offers himself afresh to us too.

DON'T KID YOURSELF

The level of self-deception that lurks in the heart of a big brother can be frightening. He is blatantly disobeying his father, who has come out personally to escort him into the banquet. His out-of-control tirade is beyond belief in a culture where to pub-licly dishonor someone was a terrible crime, hence the rabbinic saying, "It is better for a man that he should cast himself into a fiery furnace rather than that he should put his fellow to shame in public."[1]

The elder brother shamed not just anyone; he shamed his own father. He was treading a risky pathway. In the story of Esther, Queen Vashti was summoned to appear at a banquet, but she refused to enter. So incensed was her husband that Vashti was deposed, such was the level of insult and threat to his royal author-ity. Near Eastern listeners would expect a similar reaction from the father in the story—servants would be sent and the elder brother would perhaps be beaten because of his dishonorable, scandalous behavior. One ancient commentator wrote, "In his refusal to enter, the older son demonstrated maliciousness of character and mean-ness. He has no love for his brother and no appropriate respect for his father."[2]

Yet even as he commits such a blatant, hurtful crime, he pro-tests his own innocence and faithfulness: "I never disobeyed your orders." He looks back over the years and sees only unbroken faithfulness, but even as he speaks, he stands in the place of total rebellion. When we are big brothers, we fail to see our pride, our arrogance, our judgmental attitudes, and our own need for grace. When we believe that the church is only for good people, then the only way for us to legitimately stay in it is to believe that *we* are good people! If the church can't accept people who mess up, then the church can't accept you or me. But big brothers are usually the last to see this; sin is always someone else's problem.

A friend was telling me that he was struggling with bitter-ness towards another Christian, and, needing to take an air flight somewhere, he had fought feelings of anger and resentment while traveling that day. "Jeff, if that plane had gone down, I'd have gone straight to hell," he remarked ever so casually. But his comment reveals the interesting notion that his resentment could take him to hell and, therefore, his lack of resentment could take him to heaven. We'd better face the sad yet wonderful fact that our saint-liness won't buy us a second of eternity with God and that our sins won't keep us out either. We are sinners. Jesus is the great Savior. By this we are humbled, grateful, and realistic about ourselves.

AN UNHOLY FIXATION WITH STUFF

In the end, the whole argument came down to a goat, or rather, the lack of one. The only example that he could muster to prove his alleged years of slavery was the fact that Dad never gave him meat to feed his friends with. Of course, whether it's a goat, the pew we've become attached to (now taken by a newcomer or returning prodigal), the sanctuary carpet that's been stained by those folks who bring their coffee into the building, or the money that we're going to have to spend to pay for more pastoral help or a bigger building, it usually comes down to a fixation with *stuff*. When that happens, pettiness reaches an epidemic level and churches fall out as they insist on majoring on minors.

A more horrendous example of this took place in one church — a rather special church, actually — during the ceremony of the Holy Fire, so-called because it's believed that fire descends from heaven to the tomb during the ceremony. The ceremony takes place on the Saturday before Easter in the darkened tomb in the Church of the Holy Sepulcher in Jerusalem, where tradition insists that Jesus was buried. But recently another kind of fire broke out. According to various news and Internet reports, as the Greek Orthodox Patriarch and the Armenian Archbishop made their way toward the tomb, fights broke out between the priests of the two communities, with police attempting to separate them. It's not the first time that there's been trouble in the holy place. Back in 2002, a huge brawl broke out involving hundreds of the faithful. Now more than a thousand police are required to be on hand for the annual ceremony. Another fight broke out over whether a chapel door should remain open or closed. A valuable Oriental carpet extended a few inches into the Franciscans' space, so a friar cut it off with scissors. And a ladder has been parked against a wall for decades because the various denominational custodians can't agree about who should move it, an enduring monument to pernickety territorialism.

Another church voted unanimously on an expensive building program, but found itself in strong disagreement over the forty dollar purchase of used choir robes. At yet another church, a minister has been dismissed without notice for the "crimes" of asking people to respond at the end of a sermon, having a missionary speak in the Sunday morning service, and using too many illustrations during preaching. After a distinguished one hundred year history, a Baptist church in the USA split into quarters—over the position of a piano stool. Apparently the four different factions in the church can't agree about where the seat should be placed, so now they are holding separate services, each led by a different minister. None of the clergy are speaking to one another and people are afraid that violence could break out.

As we hear about all this disgraceful big brotherly behavior, we can tut-tut and quickly believe that we could never be guilty of such folly—another example of the self-deception that we've just been considering. Sometimes the sobering truth is this: the person who stares back at us in the mirror is a big brother.

Chapter 14

DOLCE: MIRROR, MIRROR

Dolce: Softly

We were delighted when a pair of starlings picked the eaves of our house to build their nest. We watched each day in awe as their woven masterpiece of twigs and moss took shape, a solid, safe haven against high winds and driving rain. It was all rather lovely until the early morning head-butting began.

Now, each sunrise we are awakened by the male starling hurtling himself against our bedroom windowpane. He peers at the glass, attacks it, momentarily recovers from what is probably a nasty headache and a corrugated beak, and then repeats the whole performance again. This goes on for about an hour, until the exhausted feathered fighter pilot pops off, presumably for an aspirin and a nap. He's not the only one who's tired. Our daily wake-up calls are turning us into a red-eyed couple who fantasize about showing our kamikaze bird friend the business end of a shotgun (don't write in to complain; I jest).

Extensive ornithological research (thirty seconds on Google) reveals that our bruised and bewildered friend is doing this because he sees his own reflection in our window, and, thinking that he's spotted a predator, launches into the flurry of attacks. He sees himself and he senses danger.

That got me thinking. As I tap-tap at my computer now, I hear once again that dull, repetitive thudding, and I wonder what *I* see when I stare into the mirror—at me. Looking beyond the mere reflection, I wonder if I tend to spot the reflection of a good, godly person called Jeff, someone who is basically upright and moral? Perhaps at times I look at myself with arrogance and pride, especially when I hear of the embarrassing failure or the unspeakable evil of another. Appalled by them and momentarily glad to be me, I become like the queen in the Snow White fairy tale, with a "mirror, mirror, on the wall, who is the fairest of them all?" attitude. I cluck at others' sins and silently pronounce that I could never, ever fail as they have failed. I become haughty and judge them harshly—but worse than that, perhaps I fool myself.

Surely you and I should realize that the reflection staring back at us is a mingling of grace and grime. God has touched our lives and made us capable of greatness and love, sensitivity and sacrifice. Yet we can also wound, betray, and perhaps be guilty even of staggering crimes. Isabel Allende describes her realization of this in her book *Paula*:

> Sometimes, when I was alone in some secret place on the hill with some time to think, I again saw the black waters of the mirrors of my childhood where Satan peered out at night, and as I leaned towards the glass, I realized, with horror, that the Evil One had my face. I was not unsullied, no one was: a monster crouched in each of us, every one of us had a dark and fiendish side. Given the conditions, could I torture and kill? Let us say, for example, that someone harmed my children ... what cruelty would I be capable of in that situation? The demons had escaped from the mirrors and were running loose through the world ...[1]

Knowing that we can each be both Beauty and Beast should make us a little more willing to realistically assess our fragilities and weaknesses, and make us a lot more gracious when others stumble. They are but fellow travelers, companions with us in the holy struggle. Together we daily fight the fallen human condition. We can, in turn, be predators and saints both. There are some humans who are stunningly and consistently evil; they take our breath away with their savage heartlessness. And there are others who turn our heads because of their selflessness and moment-by-moment sacrifices. But good and evil run parallel in us all: we are all capable of both awfulness and nobility. Purity and wickedness strive to enthrone themselves in our hearts daily. The same human being is capable of both sainthood and bedevilment—glory one day, grime the next.

The sudden awareness of the evil within all of us can be a shocking experience. An example of this is found in the story of Yehiel Dinur, an Auschwitz concentration camp survivor who was called to testify against Adolf Eichmann at his trial in 1961. When Dinur saw his oppressor in the courtroom, he fainted. He later said that his shock was caused by the realization that the Eichmann before him at the trial was not the godlike army officer who had sent millions to their death. This Eichmann, he said, was an ordinary, unremarkable man. And if this Eichmann was so ordinary, then what Eichmann had done, any man could do—even Yehiel Dinur. He was capable of acting in exactly the same way.

Pecking at my own reflection is a bad, senseless habit. But I do want to learn to look at myself with a mixture of gratitude and soberness. That will surely save me from some of sin's madness, and help me look at others with softer, kinder eyes.

Chapter 15

ORATORIO: TRUE HOLINESS

*Oratorio: An extended
cantata on a sacred subject.*

*"But when this son of yours who has squandered your property with
prostitutes comes home, you kill the fattened calf for him!"*

LUKE 15:30

The angry attack continued. It was hideous, the elder brother
thought—a party to celebrate the homecoming of his kid
brother of all things. *He threw your hard-earned cash away, he's a
loyal consort of hookers ... and now you bring out the best beef—for*
him. *How could you?*

Not only does big brother never refer to his father in famil-
ial terms; perhaps he has come to see him as his employer or, as
inferred by his speech, *slave driver.* But there's another telltale
omission. Rather than saying "my brother," he instead uses the
term "this son of yours," which not only distances himself from
the prodigal, it also carries a hint of further reproach and accusa-
tion. *He's yours, this wretch. Like father, like son. The family likeness
is obvious.*

Oblivious to his own outrageous behavior, big brother focuses
on the sins of his younger brother, real or imaginary. His conclusion is chilling: he wants nothing to do with the lad. *If he's inside
the house, then I'm fine out here.*

As the elder brother keeps his distance, he falls into the trap that
God's people seem forever vulnerable to—insisting that those who
consider themselves "holy people" keep separate from "less holy"
sinners. When that idea prevails, churches become functionally
useless, unable to fulfill their mission to a grubby world. Returning

prodigals face a cold shoulder because of their more glaring issues, and holiness becomes a system whereby the "truly sacred" are recognized by their ability to check certain "holy" boxes. Holiness quickly becomes a kind of prohibitionist purity, defined by what we *don't* do. Because no one can keep up the perfect standard for long, a pretentious atmosphere develops as the "holy" ones struggle to maintain their cover. Hence Jesus's rebuke to the hypocritical Pharisees, who had mastered the art of play acting. As we'll see, true holiness is a call to beauty and an escape from the mad, bad deal that is sin. So how has it all become so contorted?

STOP THE WORLD, I WANT TO GET ON

Some of this results from misunderstanding, at times fuelled by bad teaching. The preacher, with an authoritative, booming voice, bellows that we are called to "come out from them and be separate," — the apostle Paul's words to the church at Corinth.[1] Some Christians even refer to their lives prior to coming to faith as "when I was in the world," as if now they are somehow floating above it. But Paul's words are not a call to *physical* separation and exclusivity, but rather distinctiveness in our behavior that authenticates our claims to be followers of Jesus. Paul himself recognized that physical separation was not what was in mind: "I have written you in my letter not to associate with sexually immoral people — not at all meaning the people of this world who are immoral, or the greedy and swindlers, or idolaters. In that case you would have to leave this world."[2]

The parable of the prodigal was taught precisely because of Jesus's close proximity to sinners; he was very much "in the world" and was severely criticized for it. Jesus didn't follow the ranting preacher's application of Paul's "separation" message at all — on the contrary.

Another reason for the idea that holiness equals physical separation is a very real fear that faith will be "contaminated" by our association with the wrong kind of people. Steve Chalke illustrates wryly:

A friend of mine is the vicar of a fairly "high" Anglican Church. One Saturday morning a member of his congregation, a Church Warden, came to his door in a state of desperate panic. He invited her in to find out what was wrong and what he could do to help. As soon as they were inside the door she began her story. That morning she had been to collect a box of communion wafers for the next day's Eucharist service. She had put the wafers carefully into her handbag and caught the bus home. But when she arrived back at her house she discovered that the box had somehow opened in her bag, the wafers had spilt out and broken into countless pieces. Not knowing what to do she went straight to the vicar's house, still clutching the bag filled with the crumbs of Christ's body.

Having heard her story, my friend sympathised that it was a shame the wafers had been broken, but that it really wasn't something to get in a panic about as they could always get some more. "But you don't understand," said the woman, still noticeably agitated. Staring into the handbag at the crushed wafers, she posed the question: "Well, Reverend, it's just that ... has my handbag contaminated the host, or has the host sanctified my handbag?" The story may be light-hearted, but it illustrates a serious question for the church: Do we fear that involvement in "secular" society corrupts and contaminates us? Who is safe to include in our communities? Where do we draw the line? Should we draw a line? If we don't, will we be compromised and lose our distinctives? Standards matter! Should we withdraw and safeguard ourselves and the truth we hold?[3]

As Scripture makes clear, bad company *can* corrupt character;[4] the addict who has been embroiled in the drug culture needs to break ties that would lead him back to that hellish dependency. But beyond that, let's realize that holiness is a powerful, positive force that can change those who come into contact with it; holiness does not need to be cloistered or protected. Far from being fragile, it is able to bring wholeness where there is brokenness and scatter the forces of darkness. The leper does not make Jesus unclean, but rather is cleansed by him;[5] the Gerasene demoniac[6] is unclean for so many reasons (he lives among tombs, in Gentile territory, near swine, and is possessed by an unclean spirit). Yet he is cleansed by the power of Jesus's holy presence. The wonderful truth of the clean hallowing the unclean is continued in Paul's thinking about the believer's sanctifying effect on his or her unbelieving spouse.[7]

And then people worry about the reputation of the church. If anyone can show up, what kind of message does that send? When Bob, an alcoholic, started regularly attending a church in South London, some got worried, according to the pastor:

> A while ago I was confronted by one church member who wanted to complain about the fact that "newcomers" would stand on the church steps smoking before and after services. He was concerned that "it sends out the wrong messages." What he was really saying was that he was uncomfortable about the fact that things had become messier than they were in the "good" old days. Just last week several drunk people (and their dog!) came in to our morning service and caused absolute havoc—shouted at the preacher, spilt their drinks on the carpet and sang a verse of a very different song to those we normally sing on Sunday mornings. A few of our church members were really upset.[8]

But difficult and uncomfortable though it is, surely our reputation should line up with Jesus. He was famous for being a friend of sinners, and so should we. His insistence on befriending them in no way diluted his core values, for his decision to be around them lay at the core of his mission. Our churches are not supposed to be packed with "good" people, and we are not to be known as those who are forever looking for a "better class" of sinner to help us keep up appearances.

ROLLING OUT THE RED CARPET FOR ALL

So what is holiness, and how can a holy people be as prodigal friendly, as all-embracing, and as welcoming as Jesus? Steve Chalke calls for inclusivity:

An inclusive church will be a community open to all—a community for those who have no community. It will be an environment in which the unloved and the unlovely find refuge and belonging. It will be a home to the homeless, a family to the forgotten, a friend to the lonely and a place where the outcasts of society can enjoy life in all its fullness.

An inclusive church will not be made up of people who have got life "sorted." Instead it will almost certainly include drug users, alcoholics, people with mental health problems, homeless people, the unemployed, single mothers, people recently released from prison, prostitutes and so on. It will be a church where the imperfect are perfectly welcome. In short, it will be a home for those who need one. An inclusive church will be the kind of community to which people will want to belong.[9]

But here's the challenge: holiness—or at least mutated, deficient views of holiness—will always clash with inclusivity. If the church is called to be pure, how can we achieve that if we roll out the red carpet for notorious sinners and returning prodigals? We need to find an answer if the prodigals are to find a home to return to.

HOLINESS MATTERS

The Bible is clear—God *is* holy and he wants to make his children like him in 24/7 holy living. A few examples from Scripture of that call to holiness will suffice:

Therefore, prepare your minds for action; be self-controlled; set your hope fully on the grace to be given you when Jesus Christ is revealed. As obedient children, do not conform to the evil desires you had when you lived in ignorance. But just as he who called you is holy, so be holy in all you do; for it is written: "Be holy, because I am holy." (1 Peter 1:13-16)

Dear friends, let us purify ourselves from everything that contaminates body and spirit, perfecting holiness out of reverence for God. (2 Cor. 7:1)

What kind of people ought you to be? You ought to live holy and godly lives. (2 Peter 3:11)

Ajith Fernando states that 1400 of the 2005 verses in Paul's writings have something to say about holiness, godliness, or Christian character. This call to holiness comes from the loving heart of God, because sin is catastrophic. When humans lose their sense of the holy, they become less than human.

The Nazis knew this when they designed the death camps of the Holocaust. Not content to ferry millions into the gaping ovens, they sought to wear down and kill the Jews slowly by consistently profaning the holy in a strategy so repulsive that one writer describes it as "excremental assault."[10] In Auschwitz, there were no sanitary facilities, except one tap that Jewish women were forbidden to use.[11] Melissa Raphael writes, "The absence of sanitary facilities in the women's camp of 14,000 women was ... a deliberate way of erasing the humanity of women, condemning them to die in and as excrement. The surface of the body was broken and covered over by lice and fleas, encrusted with mud and filth, suppurating sores and boils, cracked by sunburn and frostbite."[12]

This dehumanizing strategy meant that a prisoner was never addressed by her name, but referred to as a number. Her stench and appearance further prohibited approach, touch, relationship, and the possibility of being known.[13] But her Jewishness itself was specifically fouled, with a program of routine desecration of the holy. Some women were forced to use torn-up pieces of *talles* (prayer shawls) to wear as underclothes. Others were given strips of prayer shawls to hold on their ill-fitting shoes, so that "by this means, the symbols ... of prayer were trodden into the mud, and, for those many who suffered uncontrollable diarrhea, literally shat on."[14]

The word *sheiss*, the German equivalent for the vulgar word for human excrement, was the guard's usual form of address to Jews; corpses were referred to as *scheiss-stuke* (pieces of excrement). This was a catastrophe indeed — death before death, a long, slow dying as the holy was systematically profaned. That is the purpose of sin, to ritually defile us until we can think of no worthwhile reason to live.

But the opposite of catastrophe is a "euchatastrophe," a word invented by fantasy writer J. R. R. Tolkien to describe a *good* upheaval, a eucharistic revolution. Something like it is described here in this scene from Tolkien's *Return of the King,* from the Lord of the Rings trilogy:

> "Gandalf! [Sam said] I thought you were dead! But then I thought I was dead myself. Is everything sad going to come untrue? What's happened to the world?"
>
> "A great Shadow has departed," said Gandalf, and then he laughed, and the sound was like music, or like water in a parched land; and as he listened the thought came to Sam that he had not heard laughter, the pure sound of merriment, for days upon days without count. It fell upon his ears like the echo of all the joys he had ever known. But he himself burst into tears. Then, as a sweet rain will pass down a wind of spring and the sun will shine out the clearer, his tears ceased, and his laughter welled up, and laughing he sprang from his bed.
>
> [Sam answered Gandalf] "How do I feel?" he cried. "Well, I don't know how to say it. I feel, I feel" — he waved his arms in the air — "I feel like spring after winter, and sun on the leaves; and like trumpets and harps and all the songs I have ever heard."[15]

This wondrous holiness is for all. It's not just the way of life for the passionate Christian; it is the pattern that the creator God has designed for every human life. To live a holy life is to experience what it means to be truly human. Holiness is not a dreary, morbid state, but is rather like pure, clean water; it is a refreshing delight, a true euchatastrophe.

Holiness.

It's beautiful. And the prodigal-friendly church will celebrate that beauty.

CALLED TO BEAUTIFUL HOLINESS

If holiness is beauty, then the church is called to be a beautiful model. The prodigal-friendly church is not careless morally, for that would silence her call to a lost world. She is a church of ideals and clear biblical standards; yet she is a church still in process. So the church that is prodigal friendly is both idealistic and realistic, committed to God's standards and yet unsurprised by failure. The Bible is *not* the story of surgically-enhanced people of God, their defects and gaffs airbrushed out. Instead they are shown in their splendor and stupidity, warts, as they say, and all. Check out the disciples of Jesus. As they try to build hotels on the Mount of Transfiguration, send hopeful parents packing, try to cancel the feeding of the five thousand, swing swords wildly and argue among themselves about the seating arrangements in the kingdom to come, we see an almost comical picture of this absurd wonder: God reaching his planet with the help of some good-hearted buffoons.

The church *is* a bride, but she is a bride still being prepared for her wedding. At times, her hair's a mess. Her nails aren't done. The dress needs adjusting, and there are some unwelcome bulges and a chipped tooth to repair. She is a bride still experiencing a makeover.

Her leaders and influencers *are* called to high standards. But even this is understood within the context of our mess and slow transformation. The fact that Paul called for leaders who were not married to more than one partner and were neither thugs nor drunkards[16] suggests that there were some of those kinds of people in the churches he addressed. Leaders are not called to be grinning icons who imply that they have arrived, but fellow travelers in the journey who help to lead the way. Prodigal-friendly churches will be places of truth telling and vulnerability. Leaders *are* called to be an example,[17] but that doesn't mean projecting a false image. Their example is not in some false *perfection*, but rather in the determined *direction* that they are pursuing. They can share some of their struggles redemptively, not to condone a freedom to sin, but to invite other struggling disciples into God's sanctifying work too. Only the strong and secure can be this vulnerable, for it is a sign of true maturity. When we were young, we knew that we were vulnerable, and perhaps thought that when we became adults we would grow out of vulnerability to a place of strength. But this was nothing more than dream, a false view of maturity. Being adult means that we have rejected our fairy-tale notions of being grown up and have embraced process and weakness as part of our ongoing lives.

Members of a prodigal-friendly church will both accept one another as sinners and encourage one another as saints in an atmosphere of wild holiness that laughs derisively at the stupidity of sin. Sometimes there will be tears and church discipline needed when leaders or those in places of influence systematically live lives that discredit the gospel. But even that is exercised to bring those caught napping (because of sin's seduction) out of their slumber and get their lives back. Clarity is needed if a prominent person flaunts a life of obvious, ongoing evil, such as the man in Corinth who was sleeping with his stepmother (some say it was his mother). Radical surgery was needed, but even in that situation Paul wrote again to correct the overzealousness of the discipliners, and insisted that the repentant, remorseful man be restored fully to fellowship.[18]

In practice, church discipline is only relevant to the committed core of the church. The fact that someone begins attending a public gathering of a congregation does not give that church the right to act as a moral police force in that person's life. They may come and be part of the church family for a day, a week, or five years, and yet at no point suggest that they are placing themselves under the moral leadership of the church. Biblically, authority is something that we submit ourselves to—not something imposed on us by others. Perhaps this is why the early church treated postbaptismal sins more seriously, because baptism was a very public act of allegiance to Christ, and therefore shameful behavior brought shame to his name.

In Timberline Church, those who serve in any ministry and leadership capacity agree to a covenant that expresses their desire to live in a way that pleases God. But while the core of the church needs to be strong, it must have fuzzy edges, so that anyone can travel with the redeemed community. John Drane describes the call to us to both comfort and challenge each other:

> The need of our culture (not to mention the gospel imperative itself), is for us to create a community where people can feel comfortable to belong, and then to be continuously challenging and encouraging one another in the belonging and following. Far from this being a mere accommodation of the gospel to the spirit of the age, it is actually a more biblical way of being church, deeply rooted not only in the teaching of Jesus himself, but in the fundamental Christian doctrines of creation and incarnation.[19]

HEALING THE WOUNDED IN A HOLY FIELD HOSPITAL

Although there will be victories to celebrate as we leave behind some destructive patterns of behavior, the prodigal-friendly church is not a trophy case; it's more like a hospital. One writer describes the church like this:

> In many senses the Church is a hospital—it is a place of spiritual, social, emotional, moral and psychological healing. And just as with a hospital where the patients all

suffer from different conditions, are at different levels of health and are all at different stages of the healing process, so it is with the Church. Sometimes healing takes weeks or months—sometimes it takes a lifetime. Simply visiting a hospital doesn't automatically make a sick person well, some need intensive care, others less intensive but no less important ongoing treatment or rehabilitation. A hospital is not a centre of physical perfection and neither is a church one of spiritual perfection—rather both are messy environments full of messed up people striving to be less so.[20]

I'd like to suggest that the analogy of a *field* hospital is better. In a mobile tent, in close proximity to the battle, medics work in less-than-perfect conditions to repair the bodies of those wounded in war. Ideally, when they are better, they will be able to rejoin the battle. Not everyone makes it; no one is surprised when they don't. They grieve their losses, but keep going. The cause for which they fight is too vital, the stakes too high to even think of giving up.

These analogies are important because holiness is a journey. Consider this conundrum: We are holy, we are becoming holy, and one day we will be holy. The process of holiness is rooted in what God has done, what God is doing, and what God will yet do. Our position in Christ means that we *have* been made holy as those who have been once-and-for-all set apart for God.[21] Practically, we are being changed daily as God works in our lives to make us more like Christ.[22] Ultimate, perfect sanctification will be our experience when we see Jesus in all his fullness.[23] Holiness is not about woodenly fulfilling a set of principles; it is rather being changed in the unfolding drama of daily friendship with God and God's people.

Today, the journey continues for us all. We must not be surprised if someone trips and falls, and we shouldn't be horrified at the sight of blood, or if one of the troops fails to do his duty as he should, or if he creates some disorder in the ranks. This is a field hospital; stuff like that happens here. Rowan Williams, the current Archbishop of Canterbury, describes what it means to be holy:

> A human being is holy not because he or she triumphs by will power over chaos and guilt and leads a flawless life, but because that life shows the victory of God's faithfulness *in the midst* of disorder and imperfection. The church is holy ... not because it is the gathering of the good and the well behaved, but because it speaks of the triumph of grace in the coming together of strangers and sinners, who, miraculously trust one another enough to join in common repentance and common praise ... Humanly speaking, holiness is always like this: God's endurance in the middle of our refusal of him, his capacity to meet every refusal with the gift of himself.[24]

The church that can stay faithful to the beautiful message of holiness, and yet steer through all the muck of the holiness process, will see returning prodigals find their place in the family once more. People whose lives have been shattered will be rebuilt. Earlier in this chapter, I mentioned a South London church that had a problem with drunks interrupting their services and who had endured piles of cigarette butts scattered around their front door. There's a postscript to that story:

> One of those drunks is Bob. Bob has been regularly coming to our coffee shop and spending lots of time chatting with various members of staff. When he's not drunk he's a lovely guy. But he's an alcoholic. He knows he has a problem and is seeking professional care, which we are helping to sort out for him. The reason that he had brought his friends to our morning service was that during the week he had told one of our staff that his favorite song was "Amazing Grace." For him it's not just a song. Bob has experienced amazing grace — he really does feel

like a "wretch" and consequently feels his salvation very keenly. We promised him that on Sunday we'd sing the song in church and he could stand with all of us and join in with those words that mean so much to him. Sadly, having stayed off the bottle all week, he had a drinking bout on Saturday night. Many people might have been uncomfortable about having Bob and his friends staggering about the church building causing mayhem with their dog, embarrassment with their shouting and offence with their bottles of cider. But in truth we should feel more uncomfortable if people like that don't feel that they can come into our churches. So what did we do? One of our coffee shop staff helped Bob and his friends through to another hall. We stopped what we were doing in the service as I explained briefly who Bob is, why he was with us and that we were trying to find him professional help to break free of his addiction. Finally we prayed for him. As a result, after the service another member of the congregation came to tell me about their secret addiction. And so the journey of salvation and freedom begins again.[25]

KEEP IT SIMPLE

Some churches, eager to see people make great progress in discipleship, create elaborate holiness codes, legalistic lists that everyone has to adhere to in order to show that they are authentically "spiritual." Some of the items on the list have nothing to do with the Bible, but are little more than hand-me-down ideas believed by previous generations. Many of them even fall into the category of old wives' tales. (The church in Texas that believed it was a sin for a woman to shave her legs is an extreme example.)

Challenging legalism is always a risky business, for the challenger sounds perilously close to a theological liberal. But it must be done, lest believers have the life choked out of them by these ridiculous notions. Jesus warned his disciples to avoid the leaven, or influence, of the Pharisees with their endless lists of regulations.

We saw earlier — but it's worth repeating — that legalism may go unchallenged because those who exercise it may at some point in the past have been undeniably godly people, people God blessed. To question their ideas today seems somehow disrespectful, dishonorable even. But godly people can be wrong, and the wonderful fact that God blesses any of us at any given moment is not a carte-blanche endorsement of all of our ideas.

The early church fought a constant war against the incursion of legalism, especially the notion that a Christian had to follow Jewish religious practices, such as circumcision, in order to be saved. They rightly saw that this teaching took away from the complete work of Christ and robbed believers of their freedom that has come because of the great work of the cross. To accept the burdensome teaching would have pacified the Judaizers but offended God, and would have shackled generations of believers to a Jewish holiness code that was now obsolete through Jesus. This freedom didn't come without pain, deliberation, investigation, and dialogue. The sight of the church convening in Jerusalem to resolve these matters is one of the finest sights — and greatest miracles — of the book of Acts.

Peter spoke at that gathering. He is famous for his first recorded sermon, delivered years earlier with boldness and style on the day of Pentecost. For a beginner, he did rather well back then. The sermon probably took about five minutes to deliver. He didn't have to call for any response — the crowd did that, yelling as one: *What must we do to be saved?* Three thousand swept into the beautiful family and then were baptized. The early church was on its way.

But Peter's last recorded public speech is equally fascinating, because it was given at a gathering of reconcilers. The church was desperately trying to do what we've been discussing earlier in this book — prevent a parting of a whole crowd of potential prodigals. The Judaizing virus had entered the church, and now the Council met to settle the issue: Should believers follow all the Jewish rules? They urgently needed to decide.

Peter, good Jewish boy that he was, had initially struggled with the notion that Gentiles could be saved. Then one day he drifted into a deep sleep and dreamed about a sheet being lowered before him, full of rather noxious animals.[26] The command came, "Arise and eat," which to a good, kosher-loving boy like Peter would have come as quite a shock. This was the cultural equivalent of God lowering a fully-stocked bar into a Salvation Army temperance gathering, and the voice of God saying, "Arise, you teetotalers. The drinks are on me." As Peter learned not to call unclean what God had called clean, the way was cleared for Paul's epic, world-changing ministry among the Gentiles. Peter was leading the way in making sure that the decks were cleared and that no legalistic entanglements were placed upon his Gentile brothers and sisters. "Now then," Peter said, "why do you try to test God by putting on the necks of the disciples a yoke that neither we nor our fathers have been able to bear? No! We believe it is through the grace of our Lord Jesus that we are saved, just as they are."[27]

Peter insisted on resisting the demand of voices — pious-sounding voices — that would have robbed God's people of their freedom. Indeed, to seemingly "play it safe" with legalism would have tested God. Absolutely affirming that circumcision was unnecessary and wanting to "not make it difficult" for the Gentiles, the gathering at Jerusalem tried to help oil the wheels of fellowship between Jewish and Gentile Christians and so avoid future tensions. A request was made that they make certain ethical choices about food that had been offered to idols, meat with blood in it, and sexual morality. Why pick on these three and not include instructions about stealing or lying? Commentators agree that the Council wanted to call the Gentile converts away from "typical" Gentile living and avoid potential flashpoints with their Jewish brothers and sisters. The letter was issued.

The church did some hard, dangerous work that day. As we ask tough questions about our practices, our methods, our sacred cows, the things that *we* insist are important, let's do the same. Let's keep it simple, because freedom is a beautiful sight.

BENDING THE "RULES" LIKE JOSEY BECKHAM

In my book *Lucas on Life 2*,[28] I shared the story of a woman who had begun to see that much of her life had been restricted by legalism, and who experienced an epiphany moment of freedom that was stunning to watch. I like to call her Josey Beckham, named after the famous British soccer player of that name.

It was a *beautiful* shot, the kind of heavenly volley that sends football commentators into verbal overdrive, a punt to launch a brace of slow-motion action replays. The ball rolled gently towards the player, who eyed it nervously at first. Tension crackled in the crowd. Suddenly, as if anointed by genius, the player stepped back on their right heel, and performed a coup-de-grace kick. Hands outstretched airplane-like, poise and balance perfect, foot connected perfectly with leather with a deep, solid thud, scooping it up in a bend-it-like-Beckham power drive. It was surely sheer soccer poetry. Somewhere in the distance, a huge crowd rose to their feet as one, and gave a deafening cheer. The player, lost in the moment, was oblivious to their roar of approval.

The minister looked on, staggered. This was *most* unexpected, for this perfect kick was not performed in a stadium or park, but in the main meeting hall—the sanctuary, some would call it—of a church in mid-Wales. It was late Sunday evening when it happened. Most of the congregation was enjoying that chatty cuppa-in-hand bonhomie, the warm afterglow ritual that caps ten thousand Sunday evening services. The minister watched, feeling the pleasurable tired ache that comes when the sun sets on yet another busy Sunday, enjoying the clinking sound of china and the relaxed atmosphere. The service that had just concluded had been a happy affair. There had been a refreshing cocktail of laughter and tears, and a challenge given that we should *think* about our faith, and not just keep doing the same old things simply because, well, that's what we do. Grace was in the air.

One of the children had been playing with a ball when it happened. The football rolled across the fading carpet to Josey, a sprightly lady of 70, faithful to God and this church for the past 55 years. What would she do? Perhaps a gentle rebuke about the evils of soccer playing in church buildings?

Josey was the player. She eyed the ball hungrily, and for a few seconds she was 16 years old again, and a member of the local girls soccer team. She had loved the game dearly; perhaps she was a local star. And then, as she put it, she "got saved." Fraternizing with "the world" was not encouraged, and sports were considered "worldly." To continue on the team would mean violating the prohibitionist doctrine of separation that was preached at the time. And so Josey hung up her soccer boots for the last time, and had not kicked a ball for over half a century. There was no angst, for she was not bitter about her loss. She turned her back on the game, and threw all of her energies into the life of the church.

And then that late Sunday night ball appeared before her. As Josey said later, "something from the past rose up within me." So she performed a masterful kick. The minister's mouth fell open, first with amazement, and then admiration.

"I realize now that a lot of the things that we were told were sin, weren't really," she explained later with a warm smile.

And as I heard her story, I wondered about the countless Christians that I still meet for whom faith has been less than liberating. Too often I bump into good, kind, sincere believers who are passionately committed to a message of freedom, but who have been squeezed into the painful corsets of fear by second hand, unthinking dogma. They have left spontaneity and play—and simple down-to-earth *fun*—like discarded toys of their childhood, rejected now for a stern, almost obsessive discipleship. They need to kick a ball. Build a sandcastle. Laugh out loud. Face their uncertainties; giggle on a Sunday.

As I think about Josey, I wonder if perhaps heaven is waiting for the locked up ones to get a bit more of a life. And when they take those small steps of freedom, heaven notices, and somewhere in the distance, a huge crowd rises to their feet as one, and gives a deafening cheer. And the player, lost in the moment, is oblivious to their roar of approval.

TRUE HOLINESS IS EXPRESSED THROUGH COMPASSION

Holiness is far from being a call to withdraw from the world. It is, in fact, a demand that we utterly engage it — not just with strident evangelism, but with tender, practical care. The Pharisaic big brothers measured holiness by separation *from* sinners; Jesus affirmed that the opposite was true, and that true holiness would always be expressed by compassion.

He tells the shocking story of the good Samaritan.[29] Suddenly, one considered an unclean, despised heretic is declared "good," the cultural equivalent to Jewish ears of "the good Nazi." The Samaritan's goodness is demonstrated by his caring, compassionate attitude. Those who listened to Jesus's teaching would have entirely expected the priest and the Levite to "pass by on the other side," for to be within four cubits of a dying or dead person was to render one unclean. Allowing your shadow to pass over the corpse, or passing under the shadow of a rock that overhung a corpse, would also create uncleanness.[30] But a Jew was required to stop and help a fellow *Jew* in need of aid, which would have meant that the priest and Levite would have had to take a risk. However, the Pharisaic thinking of the day would have applauded their passing by, not taking the "risk" of defilement. Jesus challenged that thinking, teaching that it is better to take chances on the side of compassion than stay in the safety of personal "cleanliness." Just as the father in the prodigal story "had compassion" on his son, so Jesus — echoing Hosea — calls for "compassion, and not sacrifice."[31]

"Holy" people, despising their world, sometimes *forget* about its needs, a tendency that angers the God who so *loves* the world. Israel made this mistake. Increasingly, as Israelite society shifted from its agricultural roots to a more urban and commercial society, the prophets cried out against the twin viruses of greed and injustice. God's law envisioned a peaceful society in which each person rested safely under his own vine and fig tree.[32] The Jews summed up a philosophy of this holistic holiness in just one word: shalom.

Shalom speaks of the peace with God that leads to peace within ourselves, peace with each other, with our environment, and between groups and nations. Shalom means much more than a cessation of war. It includes blessings such as wholeness, health, quietness of soul, preservation, and completeness. But when Israel became prosperous, a wealthy upper class developed. The old values imbedded in the law of mutual aid and sharing were replaced by selfishness and indifference to the poor. Thus Amos cried out against oppression of the poor by the rich, and against indifference toward the hungry.[33] Truly holy people can change the world. Ignoring petty laws, utterly accepting and yet lovingly compelling one another forward with words of inspiration and encouragement, they can lead the way to make poverty history, to avoid the threat of global warming, and to call people and nations to live under the "easy" yoke of Jesus.[34] By doing so, shalom can become a reality, not just a theological idea. Anything less is not biblical holiness.

Jim Wallis presents a graphic illustration of just how much the Bible has to say about the poor. A seminary student took a Bible and cut out every reference to the poor with a pair of scissors. "When the seminarian was finished that old Bible hung in threads," Wallis said. "It wouldn't hold together, it fell apart in our hands. This is our Bible — full of holes from all that we have cut out."[35]

Holiness is not retreat; it's connection and compassion.

HOLY PEOPLE ON THE MOVE

The word *holy* has taken on a musty image, implying that the holy are those who are steeped in lifeless and empty traditionalism, who are struggling to maintain the status quo in a rapidly changing world. The idea of "sainthood" evokes images of ethereal dreamers who are somewhat disconnected from the real world, so overwhelmingly irrelevant is their piety. But holiness is a dynamic attitude of wholehearted availability to the purposes of our dynamic God. We are separated *for* as well as separated *from*. Responding to change and being flexible becomes the natural stance for the genuinely holy, because rather than whining about our own preferences and potential discomforts, the priority question is always, What is God asking of us as his instruments of purpose?

We are a "separate" people, a people set apart. But this "separation" is dynamic and positive. The great news is that God partners with humanity in his ongoing agenda for the universe; we are invited to live now for something that will last forever. Change will always be on the agenda for the prodigal-friendly church, and truly holy people will respond to move forward through the marvelous mess that being holy—and becoming holy—entails.

Chapter 16

ANDANTE: SCANDALOUS
PRAISE REPORTS

Andante: Moderately slow, a walking speed.

Last week Sophie wore an almost see-through dress to church on Sunday morning, which left little to the imagination, and was a wonderful answer to prayer. In the same congregation, there were other great triumphs to celebrate. Like John, a glittering trophy of grace, who had told the minister that he was determined to soak his mother in gasoline and set her ablaze. "As sure as Jesus has saved me, she's gonna burn," he said through gritted teeth. His is no idle threat. Vintage hatred has been distilling in him for years, simmering bile that has poisoned his soul, filling his waking thoughts, fuelling his dreams. He told his pastor that he'll kill her if he can.

Praise the Lord.

And then two-year-old Emma burped loudly during the service, which triggered a round of delighted applause. Her mother, Hannah, recently received a gift of a new bottle of perfume. Each of these events is a cause for massive celebration. I learned about them during a visit to a marvelous inner-city church this last Sunday.

I nearly forgot: there's another praise report. Jimmy got baptized, shared his story about how Jesus found him, and repeatedly shouted a word beginning with *f,* one not usually used in church, during its telling.

Hallelujah.

I know what you're thinking. You're nervous. Am I, the author, at best weird, and at worst, a little warped? Relax. I'm not suggesting that we praise a good God for bad things. I can't line up with the teaching that the only decent response to being hit by financial hardship, a rotten headache, or a passing truck is to praise the Lord *for* the disaster. I refuse to thank heaven for little girls who are raped by leering predators. I'm not going to clap my hands for joy at the news that the cancer ward has another client. So why am I delighted about incidents like a skimpy dress, a budding arsonist, a cussing convert, as well as more neutral events like a burping baby and the new scent on Hannah's nightstand?

I thank God for the church of the underdressed lady, the wannabe murderer, and the cursing baptismal candidate because they have said *yes* to the mess. Reaching out in one of the poorest quarters of Dublin, Ireland, that church has decided to be a safe place for prodigals. They've committed themselves to the long-haul trip that these new disciples must take. This is a truly "seeker sensitive" church, but with a difference. Here, no one ever graduates from seeking. The saved don't stop looking, seeking light and wisdom and truth. They simply do so as followers of Jesus now, rather than meandering under their own futile steam. Here is a family, a community of laughter and tears, of bone-numbing, hope-shattering defeat, mingled with moments of giddy, laugh-out-loud joy. Together, they have walked through blue sky days of exhilarating victory and trudged through long funeral-dark winters. This little church has gathered around many gaping graves and cried their goodbyes as they sprinkled earth on caskets.

And so the fact that fiery John shared his volcanic rage with his minister demonstrates his readiness to seek help and support rather than struggle vainly to manage his anger privately. Vesuvius might not erupt as a result. He is experiencing the wonder of authentic community. Here he has permission to be a wreck without fearing that everyone else is a Cadillac. He is taking another faltering step forward, out of the numbing solitary confinement that has characterized most of his days; this is surely a reason to rejoice.

As for little Emma with the gas, she weighed in at just one pound nine ounces when she was born only twenty-three weeks into her mother's pregnancy. She doesn't have a properly-formed throat, breathes through a tracheotomy, and had three brain bleeds at birth. She has cerebral palsy. Recently she burped, which apparently is a small wonder. Here is a church that struggles together to find joy in painful places. A grin is not required, nor is a testimony that always ends with "and they all lived happily ever after." Thank God indeed.

Emma's mother is Hannah, the lady with the perfume. Her church family presented her with it as a symbolic gift on Mother's Day. A doctor caring for baby Emma said that her progress was like a miracle, that she was a "living contradiction." And so Hannah now owns a bottle of Calvin Klein's "Contradiction," a sweet-smelling reminder that a burp can be music to the ears. Prodigal-friendly churches are happy for gas to punctuate the liturgy, and for the presence of real human beings to be felt in the place.

Jimmy with the *f*-word suffers from Tourette's syndrome, so that whenever he gets excited that particularly vulgar obscenity rolls off his tongue. Jimmy's disorder means that there is an on/off switch and a volume control somewhere deep inside him, but he can't find it. He can't help his obscene tics. Jimmy is so very excited about knowing Jesus, and so he cusses up a storm. The congregation knows this, and so they beamed at his story so punctuated with profanities. They are also praying for a day when Jimmy will be relieved of his uncontrollable outbursts. Even though Jimmy knows that the congregation understands, he is deeply embarrassed by his condition. It's painful to watch someone so firmly locked in the grip of something so ugly. Freedom for Jimmy would mean that the atmosphere of the church gatherings would not be tainted by crass expletives, which would be a lot easier on visitors. Healing for Jimmy would end the need for all those careful explanations to the children, who giggle, wide-eyed at such seemingly naughty behavior from an adult. But while this congregation waits for freedom day, they accept Jimmy with a smile. He knows it.

And what of Sophie's sexy dress? A year ago, she was a dead woman, barely walking. Her life wrecked by drugs, she had lost all hope—and all her teeth—to methadone. But she bumped into a church that showed her a better way, decided to follow Jesus, and got a new heart and some dentures. Sophie is now very much alive. The potential impact of the crocheted dress was increased because Sophie was wearing only a bra and panties beneath it. The minister saw Sophie and her virtually bare midriff, and worried.

Then he laughed out loud as he realized that, until recently, Sophie had no reason to put her glad rags on for anything. Before, there were no big nights out or joyful mornings for her—just the numbing treadmill of addiction and despair, life lost in a never-ending fogbank. Now, at last, Sophie has something—or Someone—to dress up for. She'll figure out the modesty thing sooner or later. But for now, laugh with her, because Cinderella is not just a fairy tale; Sophie has been charmed by a Prince.

Chapter 17

PIANISSIMO: WINNING OVER BIG BROTHER

Pianissimo: In a very soft or quiet tone.

*"My son," the father said, "you are always with me,
and everything I have is yours. But we had to celebrate and be
glad, because this brother of yours was dead and is alive again."*

LUKE 15:31–32

The story is almost over, and yet the shock continues. In the face of such arrogant and spiteful anger, the father would be expected by those listening to the story to order his son to be beaten, brought to his senses by some quick discipline. But the pleading continues: *Please, come inside.*

There's something very wonderful about the way the father deals with his hothead of a son. When the big brother came home, he *summoned* one of the boys outside the party. The Greek word means "to call," and it creates a picture of one person standing face-to-face with another, a stance that would be consistent with the elder brother's angry and interrogative attitude.

But when the father comes out to speak to his eldest son, another word is used that means "to come alongside." It even has the same root as the word *paraclete*, which is used to identify the Holy Spirit who comes alongside as our comforter or counselor.[1] No wonder the Arabic text of this story says that "the father spoke tenderly." Now we see an arm around the shoulder, we hear words softly spoken — perhaps even whispered — so as to not create further embarrassment for big brother in front of the staring, wide-eyed banquet guests. He's already made such a fool of himself. No, the father seeks to not only win his son around, but also to protect his dignity as he does so. There's real affection in this conversation. Throughout the parable, the word *son* is used; but now, as the father says "my son," for the first time the Greek word *teknon* is introduced, meaning "my beloved son." This is the same affectionate word that a relieved Mary used to address her son Jesus when at last he was found in the temple.[2]

Throughout this book, we've seen the damage we can do when we act like big brothers. But let's remember this: big brothers are worth reaching too. At the beginning of our journey together, we met a lady who indicted Dary Northrop when the stripper Nicky and her friends showed up.

"You've ruined this church," she hissed.

"I know I have," he replied. "What are we to do ... Will you help me to love them?"

For a moment, she was silent. Conversation continued back and forth for a while; then finally, the lady spoke, her decision made. "Well," she said, "I guess we will have to do just that. We're just going to have to love them."

And that's what they did. This lady who was fast heading towards big-sister status, continued to be part of that church that became one of the fastest-growing churches in America. But none of that would have happened if Dary had not taken the time to do some "pleading" himself. Perhaps you know people trapped in a big-brother attitude, or maybe you're a leader desperately trying to create a prodigal-friendly church. There are no surefire principles of success, but are there ways to win the elder brothers?

ASKING QUESTIONS AND COMMUNICATING WELL

Elder brothers can be quite adept at complaining. But rather than just moving into defensive mode, one way of helping people understand is simply to ask them questions. Yes, it's tough that we have drunks hanging around the building, so what *should* we do? As the question is put, those who complain find themselves searching to find an appropriate solution, which requires thought rather than just reaction.

Surely many legitimate concerns could be addressed if those of us who are leaders engaged in more "preemptive" communication. The idea behind a preemptive strike is to get in first before someone else fires their missiles. Preemptive communication anticipates what concerns might surface when a church goes through a potentially challenging season, and seeks to address those issues before they are even raised. This is not to manipulate, but rather to relieve anxiety. As Jesus resolutely walked ever closer to his arrest, trial, and death, he told his disciples what he—and they—would face in Jerusalem.[3] His approach was preemptive, an attempt to prepare them for the difficulties ahead. Leaders usually debate difficult, complex decisions in board and deacon meetings for many hours. Behind those closed doors, they have the opportunity to fully explore issues and air concerns. But they should not be surprised if the congregation responds with nervous consternation when a forty-five second announcement is made about that decision on Sunday morning; the congregation has not had the privilege of being in on the journey that led to that decision. Questions will inevitably come, not because people have a bad attitude or are divisive, but because they care about the church family that they are part of. We leaders need to take time to carefully communicate and anticipate ahead of time what some of the struggles might be.

A case in point is when Timberline Church moved into its new facility. Building relocations are times of natural anxiety, and also ideal times for the big-brother spirit to strike. Some controlling types create a furor over the details, such as the color of the bathrooms. Others grow increasingly agitated because of the change in scenery. The pew that they loved to sit in for thirty years is no more. A faithful member wonders why her deceased husband's painted portrait of Jesus that hung in the foyer of the old facility hasn't been hung proudly in the new building. The change can be overwhelming in so many ways to so many people.

To help with the transition, a series of drama sketches were written and produced, and during the month prior to the big move we took an opportunity to look together as a church family at all the likely reactions that could ignite when we relocated. As we saw ourselves in the revealing mirror that drama can powerfully provide, we laughed at ourselves and our propensity for small-mindedness. We saw what mattered and what didn't, and reminded ourselves of our reasons for making the journey. The move went very smoothly.

Our communication should be similar to participants involved in a difficult expedition, like explorers cutting through uncharted territory. We must let people know that there will be difficult and challenging times, that we feel the challenges keenly too, and that we are with them in the uncertainty of the trek. Those of us who are leaders will make mistakes along the way, which we must recognize and apologize for when we take those wrong turns. We must lead with confidence, but humility, and graciously release people who are not willing to take the tough journey. Every week Timberline acknowledges (and often prays for) the other churches in our community. We work hard to ensure that visitors don't get the idea that we think we're the best outfit in town. We are people of the kingdom, not just a particular church, and as we pray "your kingdom come" and bless the other churches in the city, we avoid the insidious disease of arrogance.

DON'T RUSH THROUGH THE JUNCTION MOMENTS

Perhaps we need to allow our church to grieve for what was, as well as celebrate what is and what could be. Some people will hanker for "the good old days" when the church was smaller and more intimate, and when the messiness of being prodigal-friendly was not a problem. Let's not wound them in their grief by making aggressive comments about moving on and dumping the past. There will be junction moments when, perhaps in prayer, the church can make yet another decision to continue to be prodigal-friendly. Take your time, because choices made in seconds can affect the destiny of a person or a church for decades.

One of those junction moments took place in a church in Oregon. Led by Pastor Cap Marks, the Assembly of God church in Rogue River was experiencing wonderful growth as prodigals came home, and many young people from the drug culture found Christ. But there was a problem. Some of these enthusiastic kids would holler and whistle loudly during the worship; it was their way of expressing their adoration to the Jesus they loved. But the pastor was worried; the shrill noise was not what the congregation was used to. One Sunday morning, he gently made a statement to the church, expressing a huge welcome to the young people and appealing to the church to be patient with their unorthodox worship styles.

In the middle of his nervous statement, an elderly lady, seated right at the back of the building, rose to her feet. Cap stared at her, his mouth open. He assumed that he was toast. He was quite wrong.

"Pastor, a few weeks ago some of these kids had no hope, and their brains were messed up by drugs. We're just delighted and thrilled that they're here. Let 'em whistle."

It was a wonderful response at a crucial junction moment in the life of that church.

PUT PRODIGAL-FRIENDLY BELIEFS INTO ACTION

The wonderful sight of a changed life can speak more eloquently than a million words. Dary remembers a deacon in Timberline who went through a really tough time when his son walked away from God and became ensnared in a dangerous prodigal lifestyle. Fearing (quite wrongly) that he had disqualified himself from leadership, he offered to resign from the deacon board. His offer was rejected, however, for we are not responsible for the choices of our adult children. The man and his family were well supported through some harrowing years with prayer and words of encouragement that sustained them. Finally, the man's son decided to come back to visit the church. There he found a warm welcome and no judgment, which led him to recommit his life to Christ. The following week, the deacon stood up during the Sunday evening service and tearfully thanked the church family for their consistent generosity and support; the church was reinforced in their commitment to being prodigal-friendly, galvanized and strengthened by the power of real-life story.

One more example will suffice. Do you remember Ken, the tough guy who bumped into wonderful, welcoming Marge one Sunday morning? I didn't mention that Ken had had his life motto tattooed onto his knuckles in bold, black ink. For years his hands had shouted his philosophy — the right knuckles carried the word *off*, and the left were tattooed with a word that begins with *f*.

Ken became a Christian and had a change of heart, but he still had the same set of knuckles. Everyone who met him saw an expletive. No one in the church said anything, even when Ken began raising his hands in worship, which might have created consternation for visitors.

Unable to find work, Ken asked the church to help him. He wondered whether there was a way to get rid of those offending words, words that not only hurt his job prospects, but were no longer his life motto. A doctor in the church agreed to perform the laser surgery for free, if money could be raised to cover the cost of the hospital facilities. An offering was taken, which turned out to be the exact amount needed to pay that bill.

Dary recalls the night when Ken was baptized, his recovering hands still wrapped in plastic bags to protect them from the water: "As he came up out of the water, he held up his hands, and said, 'Now the outside matches the inside!' There wasn't a dry eye in the place. And then Ken just bellowed out, 'I'm free!'"

When prodigals come home, let's sensitively celebrate and, when appropriate, let the stories be told. Because as life changes are shared, the church will realize on a deeper level that it was for this we were born.

REFUSING TO BE CONTROLLED BY THE ELDER BROTHERS AMONG US

Elder brothers are worth winning. But in the final analysis, they cannot be allowed to cancel the party or prevent the church from being prodigal-friendly. There is kindness, but also insistence, in the father's words to his stubborn son. A lost boy had been found; a resurrection of sorts had taken place. Celebration and welcome weren't optional. They *had* to celebrate and be glad. Often elder brothers are the ones who confront, but they are never challenged themselves. It's an uncomfortable thought, but some big brothers are bullies who bluster and manipulate in order to get their own way. That is why timidity is not a positive attribute for a leader.[4] There are times when a showdown must be risked, lest the church fail in its mission and the prodigals have no place to go. A prodigal-friendly church is made up of bold people who are willing to take a difficult, but utterly worthwhile, journey with brave, courageous leaders to help steer the way.

So now only these questions remain in our story: Will big brother go inside and join in with the fun? And will the father be allowed to do, once again, what he likes in his own house?

Chapter 18

OBBLIGATIO: TURNING THE TABLES ON EXCLUSION

Obbligato: Required, indispensable.

It's a tantalizing question: Whatever happened to big brother? Before we consider it, we should pause and realize just how strongly God calls us to be an inclusive, welcoming, prodigal-friendly church. He wants his house back.

A vivid picture of God's anger at exclusivity, and his desire to welcome whomever he will welcome, is seen as Jesus cleared the temple—his Father's house.[1]

The temple area in Jerusalem has been called "thirty acres of piety and power."[2] Eighteen thousand priests and Levites manned the place. It was home to the Sanhedrin, the final Jewish authority in all religious, civil, and political matters. The Roman militia kept an eagle eye on the area, fearing that trouble might ignite there. Between five and six hundred soldiers were housed nearby.

In Jesus's day, the temple was the epicenter of Jewish national life, boasting towering walls that soared up to three hundred feet high; some large stones in the walls weighed more than thirty tons. For many, the temple was their pride and joy, an enduring symbol of national hope in a time of Roman occupation and oppression.

It was here, in the temple courts, that Jesus overturned the tables. As he swung into action, whip in hand, it surely must have seemed that a madman was on the loose. Coins were strewn over the stone floors and makeshift tables noisily tumbled; birds fluttered away in a flurry of feathers. For a while, all temple operations were suspended.

What was it that made Jesus so angry? At first glance, it seems that it was the greed of the money changers that made his pulse race. With their spiraling exchange rates and rip-off practices, these currency sharks were fleecing sincere worshipers—which certainly warranted a whipping. But there's more. Once again, his anger was really about exclusion.

Most commentators believe that the traders had set up their stalls in the court of the Gentiles.[3] It was the only place where non-Jews could gather, and it had been turned into a noisy, bustling thoroughfare, clogged by dodgy commerce. In Mark's gospel, Jesus declares that the temple had always been intended as a "house of prayer *for all nations*,"[4] but the priests had become robbers who stole the possibility of God away from the whole world. Israel was called to be a prophetic signpost to the planet, "a light to the Gentiles," but instead she acted as if she owned the franchise on God and had "shut the kingdom of heaven in [the] faces" of those who needed him most.[5]

So, astonishingly, Jesus called "time out" on the temple, angrily tossing the tables aside. The clutter had to go; it was in the way. Jesus was willing to challenge the greatest power structures and uproot and overthrow some of the most cherished aspects of heritage and tradition. Nothing, including the revered temple, was "off limits" to him.

As we search our own hearts and ask where we have been like elder brothers, let's offer God an "access all areas" pass to our lives, practices, convictions, and prejudices.

God wants his house back. He loves the prodigals and all those who have been barred and excluded. The call to be prodigal friendly is really the call to be like God, our heavenly Father. C. H. Dodd clarified the call when he wrote, "God is your Father. Become what you are, His child. Like father, like child; to live as a child of God is to treat your neighbor as God treats you ... to imitate in one's behavior the quality and direction of God's activity."[6]

Are we willing to be those who do what God does—love the prodigals unreservedly? Will we help clear the clutter away that bars their homecoming? God will help us if we are willing.

As David Hubbard has put it, "In a massive conspiracy of grace, Father, Son and Spirit have plotted together to turn our lives around."[7]

Let's say yes to *his* plan.

Chapter 19

CODA: AND THEY ALL LIVED . . .

Coda: The closing section of a movement.

"He was lost and is found."
LUKE 15:32

It's wonderful or utterly infuriating, depending on how you view these things. You rent a movie, find yourself totally engrossed in the plot—but then the ending leaves you completely dissatisfied. There are simply too many unanswered questions, a whole host of loose ends that the screenwriter didn't bother to tie up.

These days you can choose your own ending. It's now possible, through DVD technology, to select the destiny of the characters. Do you want them happy or sad? Will the ending be conclusive or mysterious? *Press that button now, please.*

Jesus used the "choose your own ending" technique thousands of years before Hollywood ever came up with the idea. When it comes to being a big brother and part of a prodigal-friendly church—or not—we are invited by Jesus to write our own endings.

SUDDENLY . . .

It has all come to a head. The partygoers might have craned their necks forward in an attempt to hear what the father was whispering to his oldest son. The band is still frozen in silence, wondering whether they should start playing again to cover the embarrassing pause. Now they are poised to either pack up and go home, or strike up a merry tune to welcome big brother into the house. The guests are motionless, amazed at the grace of the father, shocked by the rudeness of his elder son, and waiting for his response.

But as Jesus's story ends, we never know whether the elder brother tearfully embraced his father and made his way into the party—or stomped away to sulk in the fields for an hour or two. The Pharisees at the back of the crowd listened, eyes narrowed, knowing that Jesus was asking, How will this end *with you*? What should be done with sinners? Will you see that you, elder brothers, are sinners too? Because if I can't eat with sinners, then I can't eat with you.

But there is another question implied in the cliff-hanger ending of this story. It had all begun with the Pharisees' intense criticism of Jesus. Now, having heard him out, what would they do with him, the one whom they rightly tagged as the friend of sinners? Would they carefully ponder his words and perhaps begin to see that much of what they were doing was useless, destructive religion? Or would they fight him all the harder as he continued to love those they hated?

Their response was mixed.

We have no idea if any of the Pharisees that heard Jesus tell this story were those spoken of later in the Bible narrative. What is sure is that some of their number rejected Jesus and helped in the conspiracy that led to his death.

If their response was anything to go by, the story would have ended like this:

"And the elder brother, enraged at his father, picked up a piece of wood, and struck him with it. The father died." Or, as we read in John's gospel, "the chief priests and Pharisees had given orders that if anyone found out where Jesus was, he should report it so that they might arrest him."[1] And again, "Judas came to the grove, guiding a detachment of soldiers and some officials from the chief priests and Pharisees. They were carrying torches, lanterns and weapons."[2]

But there were other Pharisees who did become followers of Jesus, like those believers who are described in the book of Acts.[3] Sadly, as Acts shows, their big-brother antics continued after their conversion, and they created a fair amount of havoc in the church.

But there was another Pharisee, one who definitely was not in the crowd when Jesus told the wonderful parable. Yet he is incredible proof that big brothers *can* change. He was that firebrand Saul, a retired Pharisee[4] and a man who became one of the greatest champions of freedom and grace in the history of the Christian church.

Big brothers *can* come home and take their place at the party. And as the apostle Paul demonstrated, the elder brothers, touched by the father's grace-kiss on their cheeks, can help create an exuberant, laugh-out-loud welcome for the prodigals, when they, at last, make their way home too. May the prodigals hear the sound of merriment and music as they return, and be surprised to find a red carpet of welcome rolled out to greet their homecomings.

Look. The conductor taps his music stand, his baton raised. *Instruments at the ready, please.* The concert continues.

CHAPTER 1: OVERTURE: GRACE AND MR. PERLMAN

1. *The Lutheran Hymnal* (St. Louis: Concordia Publishing House, 1941).
2. Also quoted in Chick Yuill, *Others* (Milton Keynes: Authentic Media, 2007), 76.
3. The Prodigal-Friendly Church Conference, organized by Spring Harvest UK, November 2005, with Rob Parsons, Dary Northrop, Jeff Lucas, Nicky Gumble, and others.
4. Hosea 11:8
5. Psalm 78:40–41

CHAPTER 2: DISSONANCE: THE MUTTERERS

1. Common Worship, Holy Communion Eucharistic Prayer D, Archbishops' Council of the Church of England, 2000.

CHAPTER 3: INTERMEZZO: DINING WITH THE PRODIGAL ZACCHAEUS

1. Donald Kraybill, *The Upside Down Kingdom* (Scottdale, Penn.: Herald Press, 1990), 224.
2. Haim Hermann Cohn, *The Trial and Death of Jesus* (Jersey City, N. J.: KTAV, 1980), 6.
3. For example, Luke 5:30
4. Luke 18:10 ff.
5. Marcus Borg, *Jesus: Conflict, Holiness and Politics* (New York: Trinity Press International, 1984), 99.
6. Ibid., 100.
7. Luke 19:9; 18:14
8. D. E. Nineham, *St. Mark* (London, Penguin Books, 1969), 95.
9. Borg, *Jesus: Conflict, Holiness and Politics*, 96.
10. Catherine Mowry LaCugna, *God for Us: The Trinity and the Christian Life* (San Francisco: HarperCollins, 1991), 401.

CHAPTER 4: MANCANDO: ARE WE PREVENTING A PARTING?

1. Kenneth E. Bailey, *Finding the Lost Cultural Keys to Luke 15* (St. Louis: Concordia, 1992), 112.

2. Ibn al-Salibi, *The Book of Unique Pearls of Interpretation of the New Testament,* written in Syriac, 1150 (Cairo: 'Abd al-Masih as Dawalani, 1914).

3. Bailey, *Finding the Lost Cultural Keys to Luke 15,* 114.

4. I. Sa'id, *Commentary on the Gospel of Luke* (Beirut: Near East Council of Churches, 1970), 321.

5. Deuteronomy 21:17 speaks of the double portion being the right of the firstborn, although the context of this passage is a multiple marriage situation where there has been an unhappy first union.

6. William F. Arndt and F. Wilbur Gingrich, *A Greek English Lexicon of the New Testament and other Early Christian Literature* (Chicago: University of Chicago, 1957), 789.

7. Bailey, *Finding the Lost Cultural Keys to Luke 15,* 122.

8. Kenneth E. Bailey, *The Cross and the Prodigal* (Downers Grove: Inter-Varsity, 2005), 45.

9. 2 Corinthians 5:18

10. Bruce Chatwin, *The Songlines* (London: Picador, 1987), 72.

11. C. S. Lewis, *The Last Battle* (New York: Macmillan, 1970), 184.

12. This famous story is quoted in Donald McCullough, *The Trivialization of God* (Colorado Springs: NavPress, 1995), 66.

13. *Mr. Holland's Opus,* DVD, directed by Stephen Herek (Burbank, Calif.: Buena Vista Home Entertainment/Hollywood Pictures, 1995).

14. As quoted in John Martin, "Rwanda: Why?", *Transformation* 12:2 (1995): 2.

15. Roger Bowen, "Revivalism and Ethnic Conflict: Questions from Rwanda," *Transformation* 12:2 (1995): 17.

16. Mark Green and Tracy Cottrell, eds., *Let my People Grow: Reflections on Making Disciples Who Make a Difference in Today's World* (Milton Keynes: Authentic Media, 2006), 22.

17. Simon Jones, *Why Bother with Church?* (Nottingham: InterVarsity, 2001), 39.

18. Green and Cottrell, *Let my People Grow,* 24.

19. As quoted in John P. Diggins, *The Lost Soul of American Politics* (New York: Basic, 1984), 7.

20. As quoted in Chris Blake, *Searching for a God to Love* (Nashville: Thomas Nelson, 2000).

21. C. S. Lewis, *The Horse and His Boy* (Middlesex: Puffin, 1954), 167–69.

22. Alan Kreider, "Baptism, Catechism, and the Eclipse of Jesus' Teaching in Early Christianity," *Tyndale Bulletin* 47 (1996): 316–18.

23. Saint Augustine, *De Catechizandis Rudibus* (12.17).
24. Michael Dujarier, *A History of the Catechumenate* 64 (New York: Sadlier, 1979), who notes, "it usually lasted three years."
25. *Apostolic Tradition* (39:1–2; see also 18:1–5; 19:1–2).

CHAPTER 5: SERENADE: AN UNCOMMON HOMECOMING

1. *Genesis*, vols. 1–2, *Midrash Rabbah*, eds. H. Freedman and Maurice Simon (New York: Soncino Press, 1983).
2. Ben Sirach, quoted in Kenneth E. Bailey, *Finding the Lost Cultural Keys to Luke 15* (St. Louis: Concordia, 1992), 121.
3. Ibid., 144.
4. Ibid., 145 (Isaiah 47:1–3 translated by Kenneth E. Bailey).
5. Romans 5:8
6. Ephesians 2:17
7. The Greek word used for the ring here is *daktylios*, a word used forty-five times in the Greek translation of the Old Testament. It comes from a root word in the Hebrew meaning "to sink into," as in the use of a signet ring to impress and stamp documents.
8. Acts 7:33
9. Steve Chalke and Anthony Watkis, *Intelligent Church* (Grand Rapids: Zondervan, 2006), 42.
10. Chick Yuill, *Others* (Milton Keynes: Authentic Media, 2007), 45.
11. Ibid., 67.
12. Exodus 10:16

CHAPTER 6: INTERMEZZO: THE VERY BEST FOR THE WORST OF SINNERS

1. Acts 7:54–8:1
2. Acts 26:10a, 11
3. Acts 26:10b
4. Galatians 2:9

CHAPTER 7: SUBITO: THE SUDDEN RETURN OF THE "GOOD GUY"

1. Matthew 12:24
2. Some scholars suggest that the Pharisees were based only in Jerusalem. N. T. Wright disputes this in *The Challenge of Jesus* (London: SPCK, 2000), 37.
3. Philo, usually known as Philo the Jew (Philo Judaeus) or Philo of Alexandria (a city in Egypt with a large Jewish Diaspora population in Greco-Roman times), lived from about 20 BC to about AD 50. He is one

of the most important Jewish authors of the Second Temple period of Judaism and was a contemporary of both Jesus and Paul. N. T. Wright, *The Challenge of Jesus* (London: SPCK, 2000), 37.

4. Marcus Borg, *Jesus: Conflict, Holiness and Politics* (New York: Trinity Press International, 1984), 96. Others have made this point too.

5. Matthew 15:2

6. Exodus 30:20

7. Deuteronomy 21:1–9

8. Acts 8:1

9. Philippians 3:6

10. B. Stanley, *The Bible and the Flag* (Leicester: Apollos, 1990), 104.

CHAPTER 9: GALLIARD: FROM PARTING TO PARTYING

1. Quoted in Chris Blake, *Searching for a God to Love* (Nashville: Thomas Nelson, 2000), 57.

2. 1 Samuel 28:24–25

3. Genesis 18:1–8

4. Michael Griffiths, *Cinderella with Amnesia* (Nottingham: InterVarsity, 1975), 23.

5. Ephesians 6:10–17

6. 1 Corinthians 12, 14

7. Jeff Lucas, *Will Your Prodigal Come Home?* (Grand Rapids: Zondervan, 2007), 152–53.

8. Deuteronomy 14:25–26

9. Zephaniah 3:17

10. Luke 15:10

11. Luke 15:5–6

12. Luke 15:9

13. As quoted in Lucas, *Will Your Prodigal Come Home?*, 155.

14. From the *Règle Orientale*, quoted in Jacques LeGoff, "Laughter in the Middle Ages," *A Cultural History of Humour: From Antiquity to the Present Day*, eds. J. Bremmer and H. Roodenburg (Cambridge: Polity Press, 1997), 40–53.

15. Patrologia Graeca 44: 645c / Gregorii Nyssani 1962: 310.

16. Penthos: La doctrine de la componction dans l'Orient Chre'tien (Orientalia Christiana Analecta by, Ire' ne' e Hausherr (Rome: Pont. Institutum Orientalium Studiorum, 1944), 132.

17. Le rire, les larmes et l'humour chez les moines d'E' gypte. In A. Guillaumont (ed.), E'tudes sur la spiritualite' de l'Orient Chre'tien by Antoine

Guillaumont, 1996 [1986] (Spiritualite′ Orientale 66). Be′ grolles-en-Mauges (France: Abbaye de Bellefontaine), 93–112.

18. Jorge, the famous enemy of laughter in Umberto Eco's *The Name of the Rose*, describes laughter as "diurnal pollution." *The Name of the Rose*, trans. W. Weaver (London: Secker and Warburg, 1983), 474.

19. Blake, *Searching for a God to Love*, 55.

20. N. T. Wright, *The Challenge of Jesus* (Nottingham, SPCK, 2000), 27.

21. Graham Tomlin, *The Provocative Church* (Cleveland: Pilgrim Press, 2002), 31.

22. Steve Chalke and Anthony Watkis, *Intelligent Church* (Grand Rapids: Zondervan, 2006), 45.

23. Tony Campolo, *Who Switched the Price Tags?* (Nashville: Word, 1986), 134.

24. Griffiths, *Cinderella with Amnesia*, 7.

CHAPTER 11: STACCATO: AN ANGRY YOUNG MAN COMES HOME

1. Luke's usual word for servant, *doulos*, used twenty-seven times, is not used here. The Arabic translation is "young boy."

2. Ibn al-Tayyib, *The Interpretation of the Four Gospels*, rev. Yusif Manqariyus (Cairo: 1908, 276).

3. Exodus 3:14

4. Mark 10:13–16

5. Matthew 16:21–23

6. Jonah 4:1–4

7. Matthew 26:6–13

8. Romans 14

9. Sally Magnusson, *The Flying Scotsman* (London: Quartet Books, 1981), quoted in Chick Yuill, *Others* (Milton Keynes: Authentic Media, 2007), 34.

CHAPTER 13: PIZZICATO: THE NEW FAMILY PRODIGAL

1. Kenneth E. Bailey, *Finding the Lost Cultural Keys to Luke 15* (St. Louis: Concordia, 1992), 171.

2. Ibn al-Tayyib, AD 1043, Tafsir II, 186.

CHAPTER 14: DOLCE: MIRROR, MIRROR

1. Isabel Allende and Margaret Sayer Peden, *Paula* (New York: Harper-Collins, 1995), 57.

CHAPTER 15: ORATORIO: TRUE HOLINESS

1. 2 Corinthians 6:17
2. 1 Corinthians 5:9–10
3. Steve Chalke, *Intelligent Church* (Grand Rapids: Zondervan, 2006), 31.
4. 1 Corinthians 15:33
5. Mark 1:40–45
6. Mark 5:1–20
7. 1 Corinthians 7:12–14
8. Steve Chalke and Anthony Watkis, *Intelligent Church* (Grand Rapids: Zondervan, 2006), 43.
9. Ibid., 55.
10. Terrence Des Pres, *The Survivor: An Anatomy of Life in the Death Camps* (Oxford: Oxford Univ. Press, 1976), 53, 57, 66.
11. Pelagia Lewinska, "Twenty Months at Auschwitz," in *Different Voices: Women and the Holocaust*, eds. Carol Rittner and John Roth (New York: Paragon, 1973), 87.
12. Melissa Raphael, "Holiness in extremis: Jewish Women's Resistance to the Profane in Auschwitz" in *Holiness Past and Present*, ed. Stephen Barton (New York: T & T Clark, 2003), 381.
13. Livia Bitton-Jackson, *I Have Lived a Thousand Years: Growing Up in the Holocaust* (London: Simon and Schuster, 1999), 83, 92.
14. Melissa Raphael, "Holiness in extremis: Jewish Women's Resistance to the Profane in Auschwitz" in *Holiness Past and Present*, ed. Stephen Barton (New York: T & T Clark, 2003), 386.
15. J. R. R. Tolkien, *The Return of the King* (New York: Ballantine, 1965), 283.
16. 1 Timothy 3:1–7
17. 1 Timothy 4:12
18. 2 Corinthians 2:5–11
19. As quoted in Chick Yuill, *Others* (Milton Keynes: Authentic Media, 2007), 114.
20. Chalke and Watkis, *Intelligent Church*, 22.
21. 1 Corinthians 1:2; 6:9–11; Hebrews 10:10
22. John 17:17; 2 Corinthians 3:18; 7:1
23. 1 John 3:2
24. Rowan Williams, *Open to Judgment: Sermons and Addresses* (London: Darton, Longman and Todd, 1994), 256.
25. Chalke and Watkis, *Intelligent Church*, 119.
26. Acts 10:9–16

27. Acts 15:10–11
28. Jeff Lucas, *Lucas on Life 2* (Milton Keynes: Authentic Media, 2004).
29. Luke 10:30–37
30. J. N. D. Darrett, *Law in the New Testament* (London: Darton, Longman and Todd, 1970), 208–227.
31. Hosea 6:6; Matthew 9:13
32. 1 Kings 4:25; Micah 4:4
33. Amos 2:6–7; 6:3–6; 8:6
34. Matthew 11:29–30
35. Jim Wallis, *The Soul of Politics* (New York: New Press, 1994), 163.

CHAPTER 17: PIANISSIMO: WINNING OVER BIG BROTHER

1. John 14:16
2. Luke 2:48
3. Matthew 20:17–19
4. 2 Timothy 1:7

CHAPTER 18: OBBLIGATO: TURNING THE TABLES ON EXCLUSION

1. Mark 11:12–19
2. Donald Kraybill, *The Upside Down Kingdom* (Scottdale, Penn.: Herald Press, 1990), 61.
3. Others contest this, notably Marcus Borg.
4. Isaiah 56:7; Mark 11:17 (emphasis added)
5. Matthew 23:13
6. C. H. Dodd, *The Founder of Christianity* (New York: Macmillan, 1970), 63–65.
7. David Hubbard, *The Holy Spirit in Today's World* (Waco, Tex.: Word, 1973), 29.

CHAPTER 19: CODA: AND THEY ALL LIVED . . .

1. John 11:57
2. John 18:3
3. Acts 15:5
4. Philippians 3:5

Will Your Prodigal Come Home?

An Honest Discussion of Struggle & Hope

Jeff Lucas

If you have had your heart broken by a prodigal, you know the pain of being hurt or disappointed by a loved one ... and the utter despair of seeing them turn away from Christ and the cross. In *Will Your Prodigal Come Home?* author Jeff Lucas delivers a message that is both challenging and comforting as he outlines the chaotic situations and emotions that families of prodigals face.

Lucas acknowledges that every prodigal is different. Some have defied God. Some are lured by drugs, alcohol, or crime. Others have drifted until the emotional and physical distance feels unbearable. Still others are in church pews, with hearts closed to Jesus. Clearly, there are no easy answers. But through understanding, insight into the emotions that form within families, and an acknowledgment of the power of prayer, this book outlines a solid approach to help guide your prodigal home and to help you keep your own faith as you wait.

Softcover: 0-310-26725-0

Pick up a copy today at your favorite bookstore!